THE NEXT DAY

A Graphic Novella

POP SANDBOX

PRODUCTION
AND
PUBLISHING

The Next Day: A Graphic Novella
Produced and published by Pop Sandbox Inc.

Pop Sandbox Inc.
PO Box 16017
1260 Dundas St W
Toronto, ON M6J 3W2
www.popsandbox.com

First edition: 2011
ISBN: 978-0-9864884-1-2
Printed in Canada

10 9 8 7 6 5 4 3 2 1

Library and Archives Canada Cataloguing in Publication
data available upon request to the publisher.

Distributed in Canada by:
Raincoast Books
9050 Shaughnessy St
Vancouver, BC V6P 6E5
Orders: 1.800.663 5714

The Pop Sandbox logo was created by Seth and
developed from initial concepts by Jason Gilmore.

Produced by
Alex Jansen & Pop Sandbox

Written by
Paul Peterson & Jason Gilmore

Illustrated by
John Porcellino

———————————————————————————

Edited by
Richard Poplak & Alex Jansen

Published by
Pop Sandbox

This graphic novella is built from intimate
interviews with four people who have
attempted suicide. It includes descriptions
of actual attempts and traumatic events
that may be upsetting to some readers.

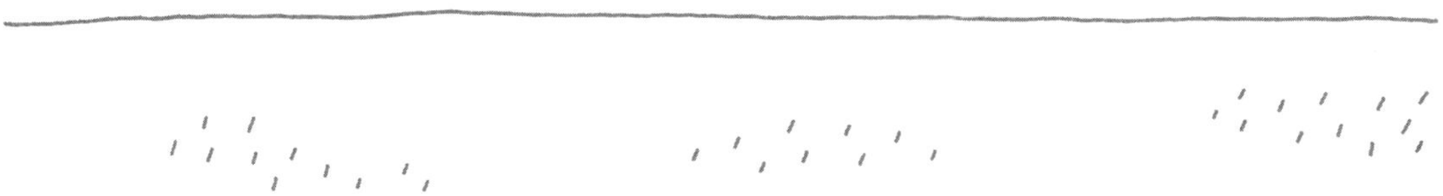

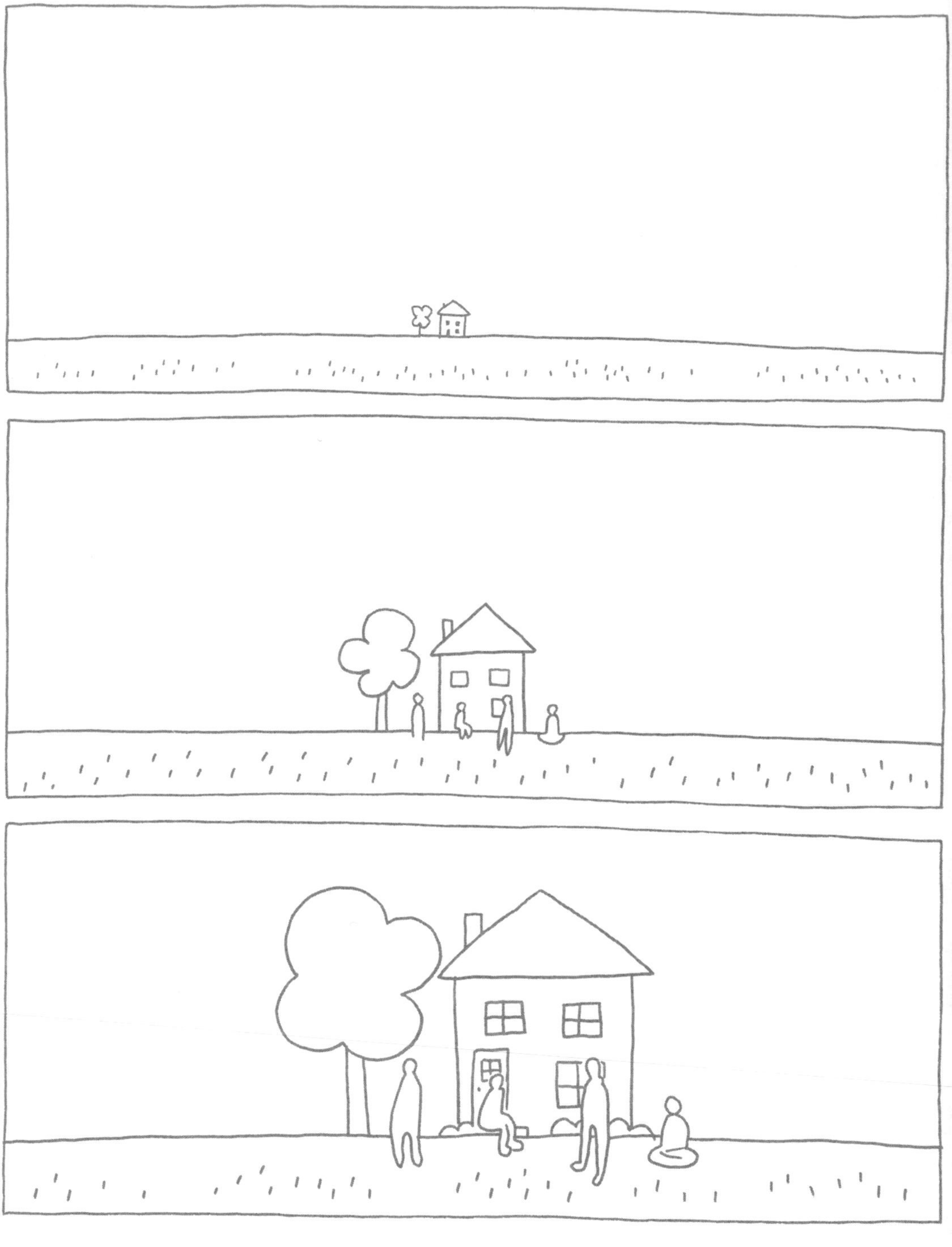

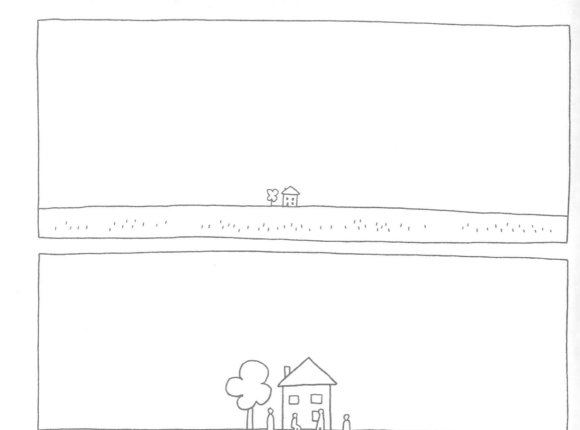

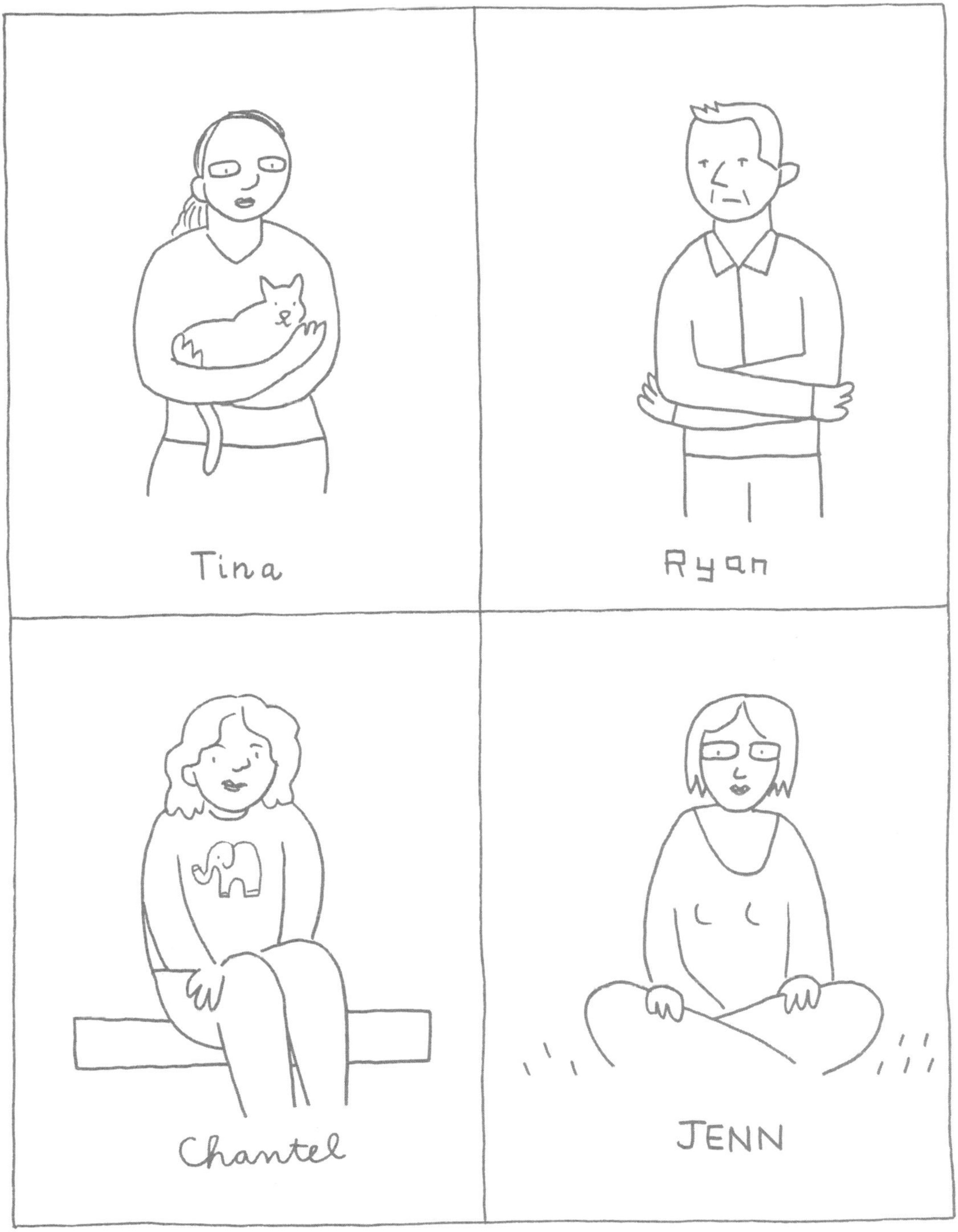
Tina
Ryan
Chantel
JENN

The Day of...

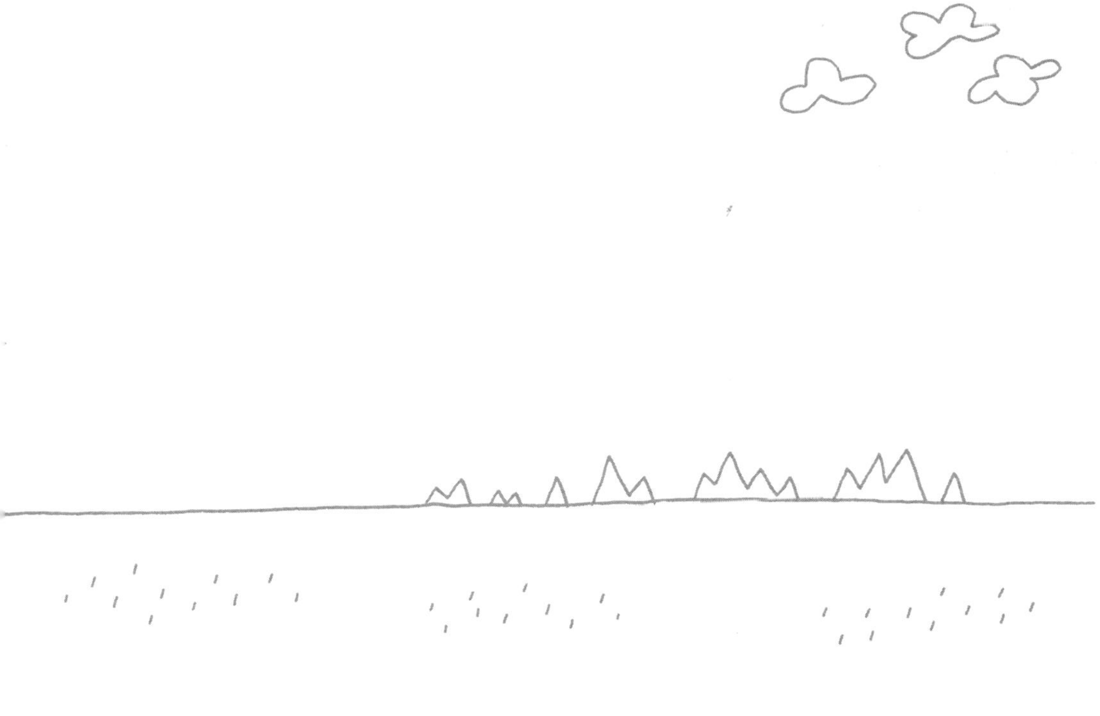

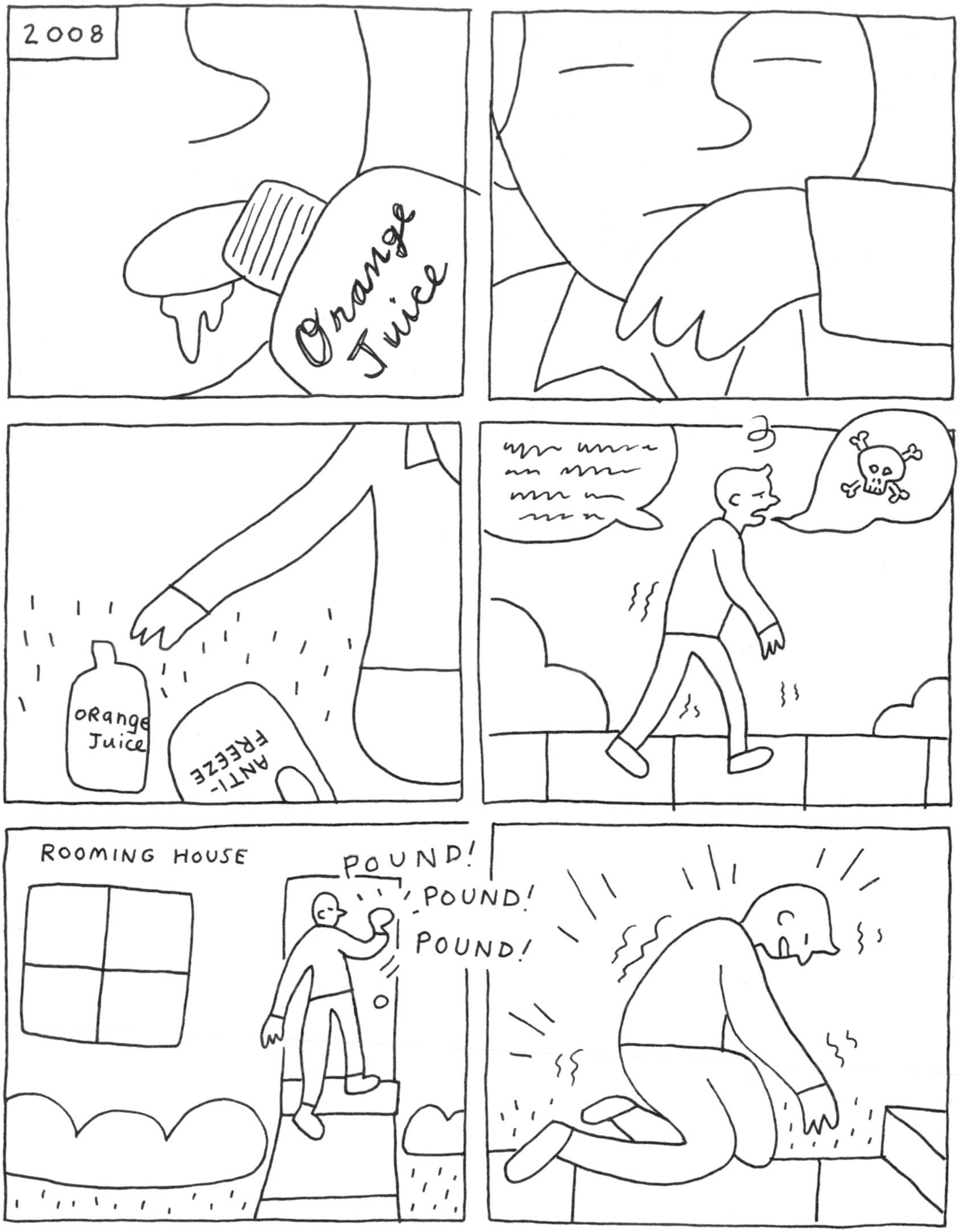
2008
Orange Juice
Orange Juice
ANTI-FREEZE
ROOMING HOUSE
POUND!
POUND!
POUND!

Ryan

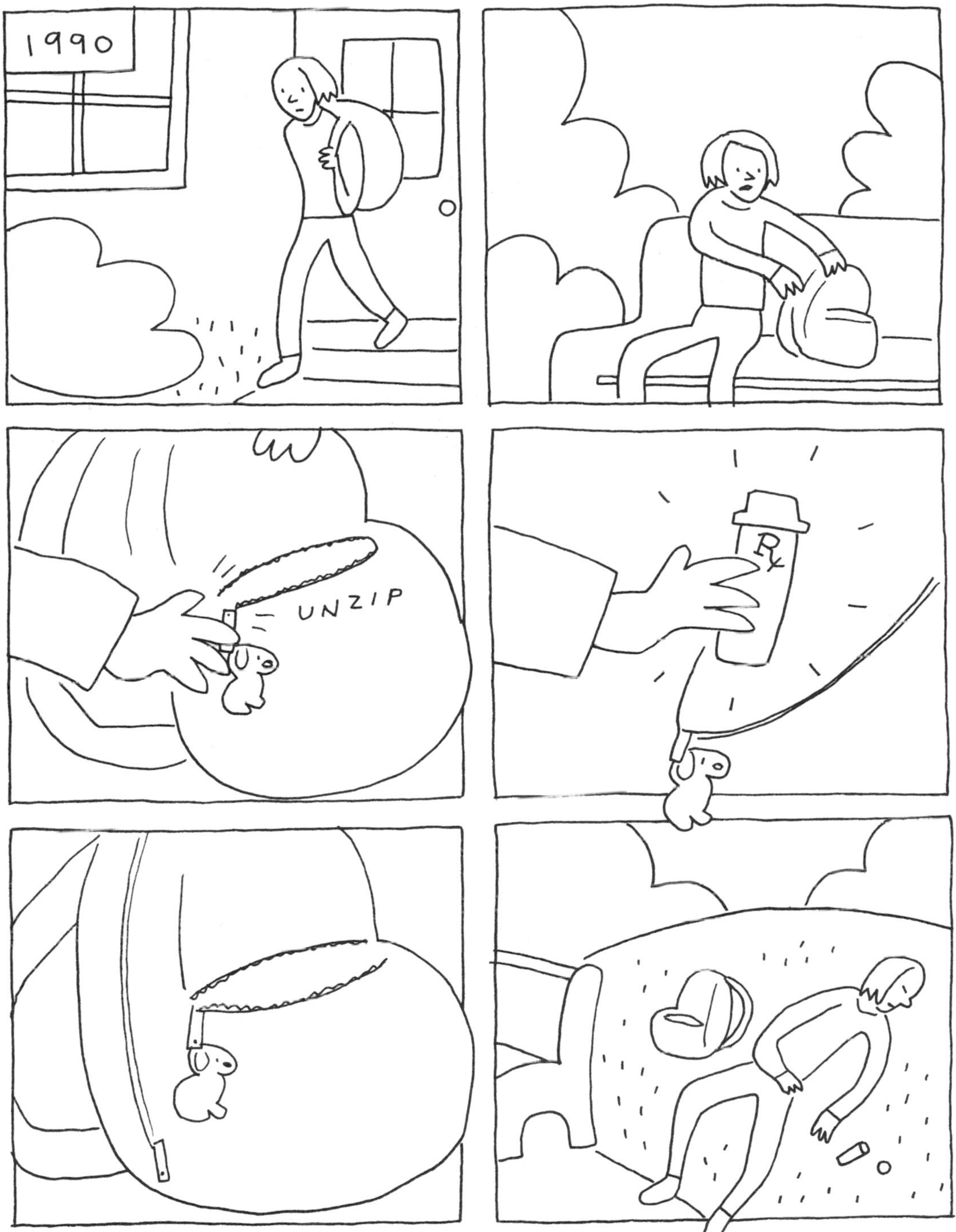
1990
UNZIP
R

JENN

1995
BAR
SOB
SOB
SLIDE
CLATTER!

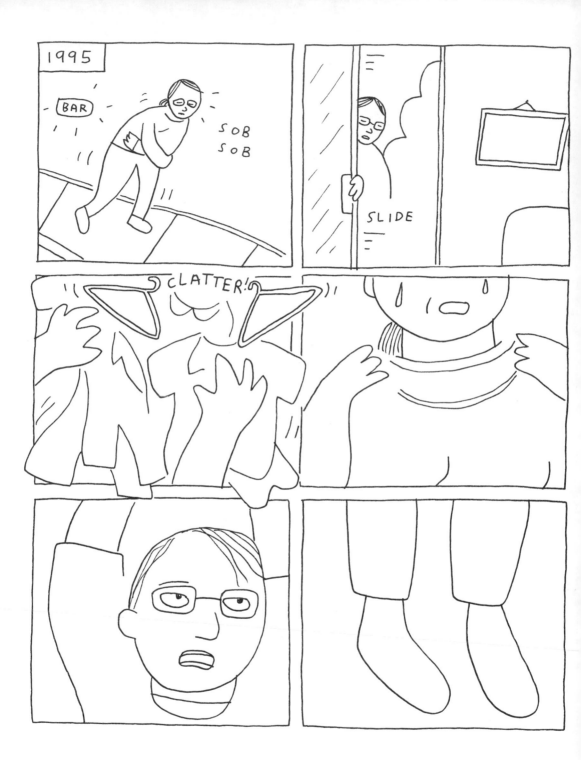

Tina

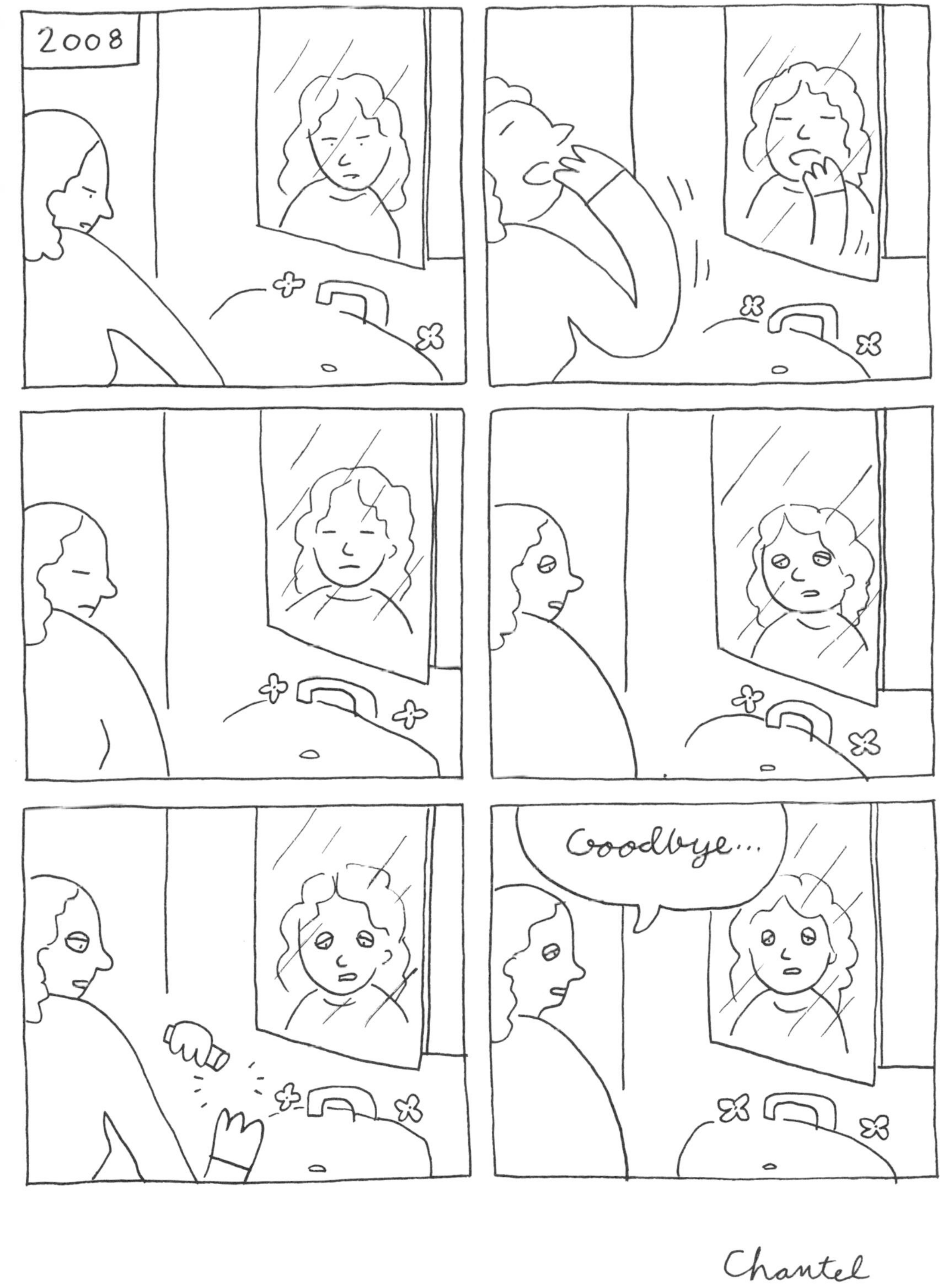
2008
Goodbye...

Chantel

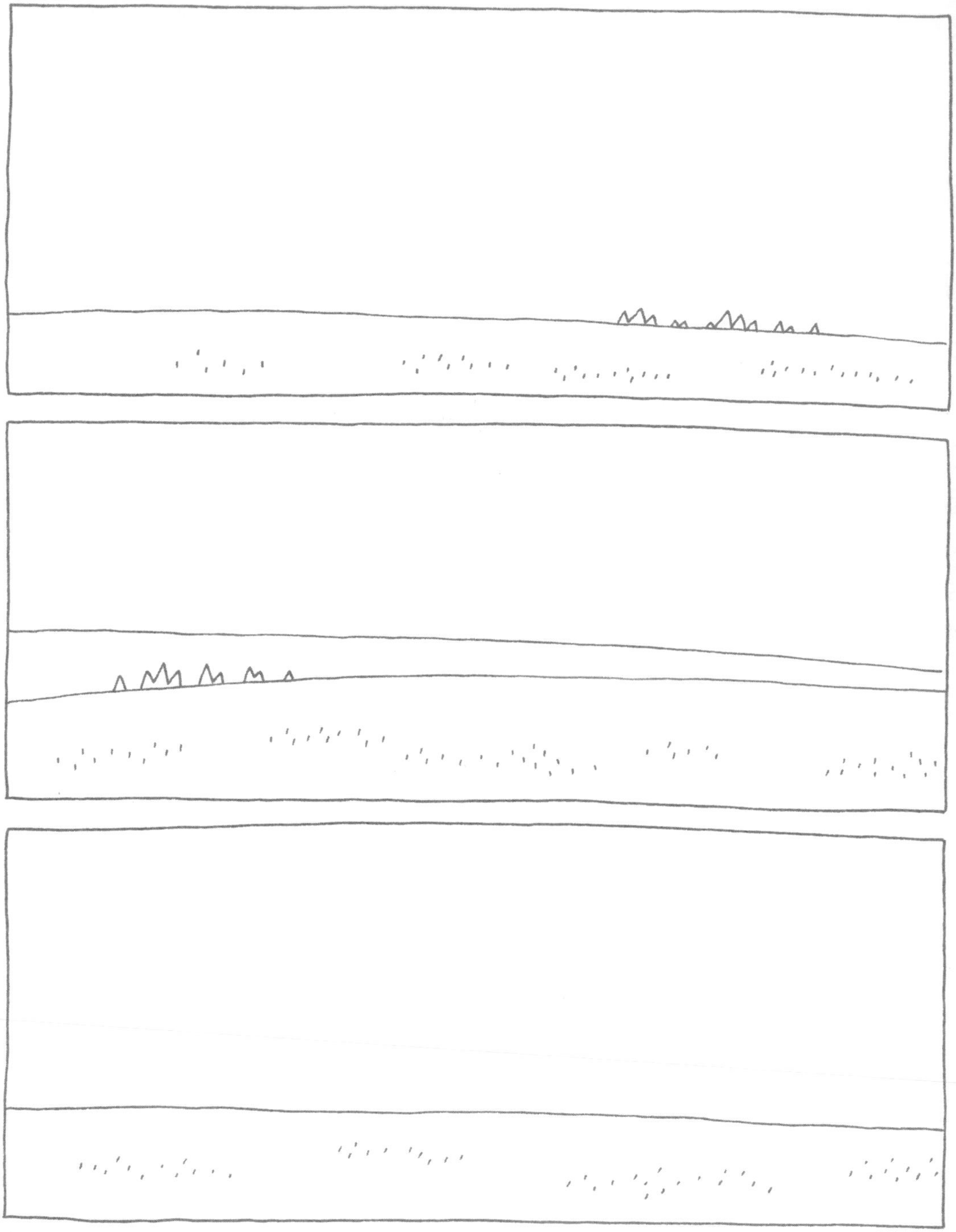

The Days Before...

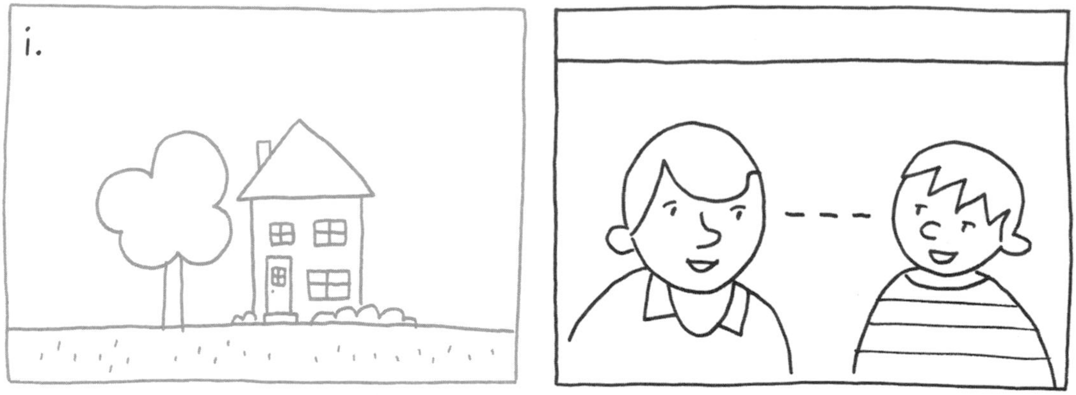
i.

I loved the home I grew up in.

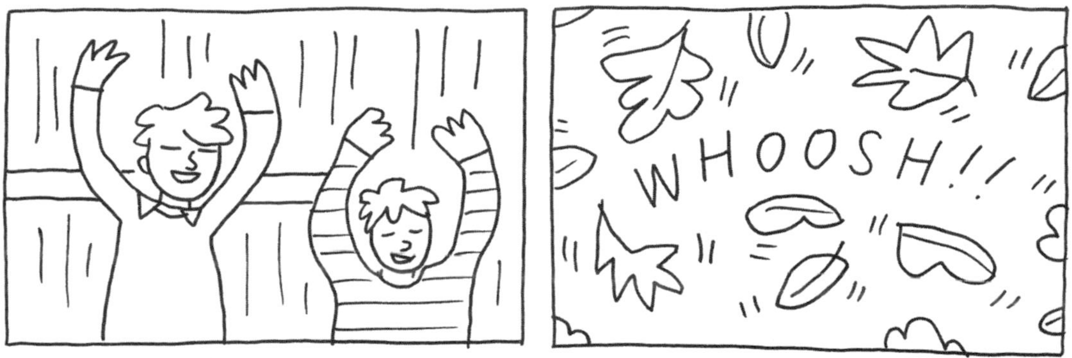
WHOOSH!!

I only lived there from the age of 7 until the age of 12, but that was still the house I grew up in.

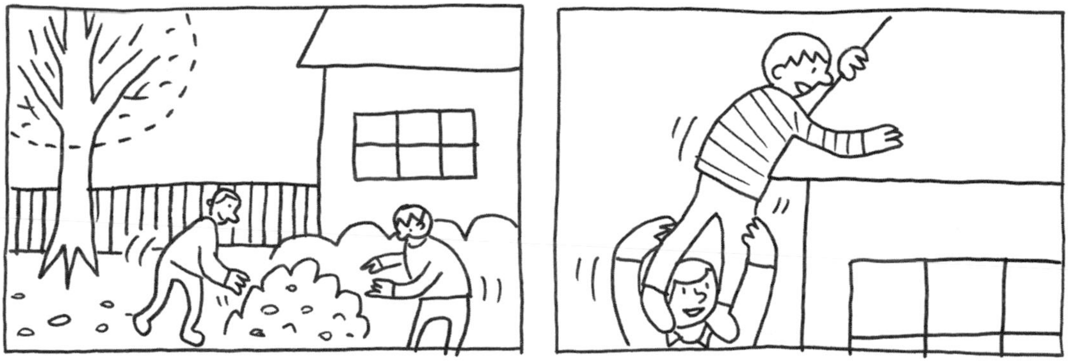

Because after that, there was the divorce, and life became extremely messy...

Ryan

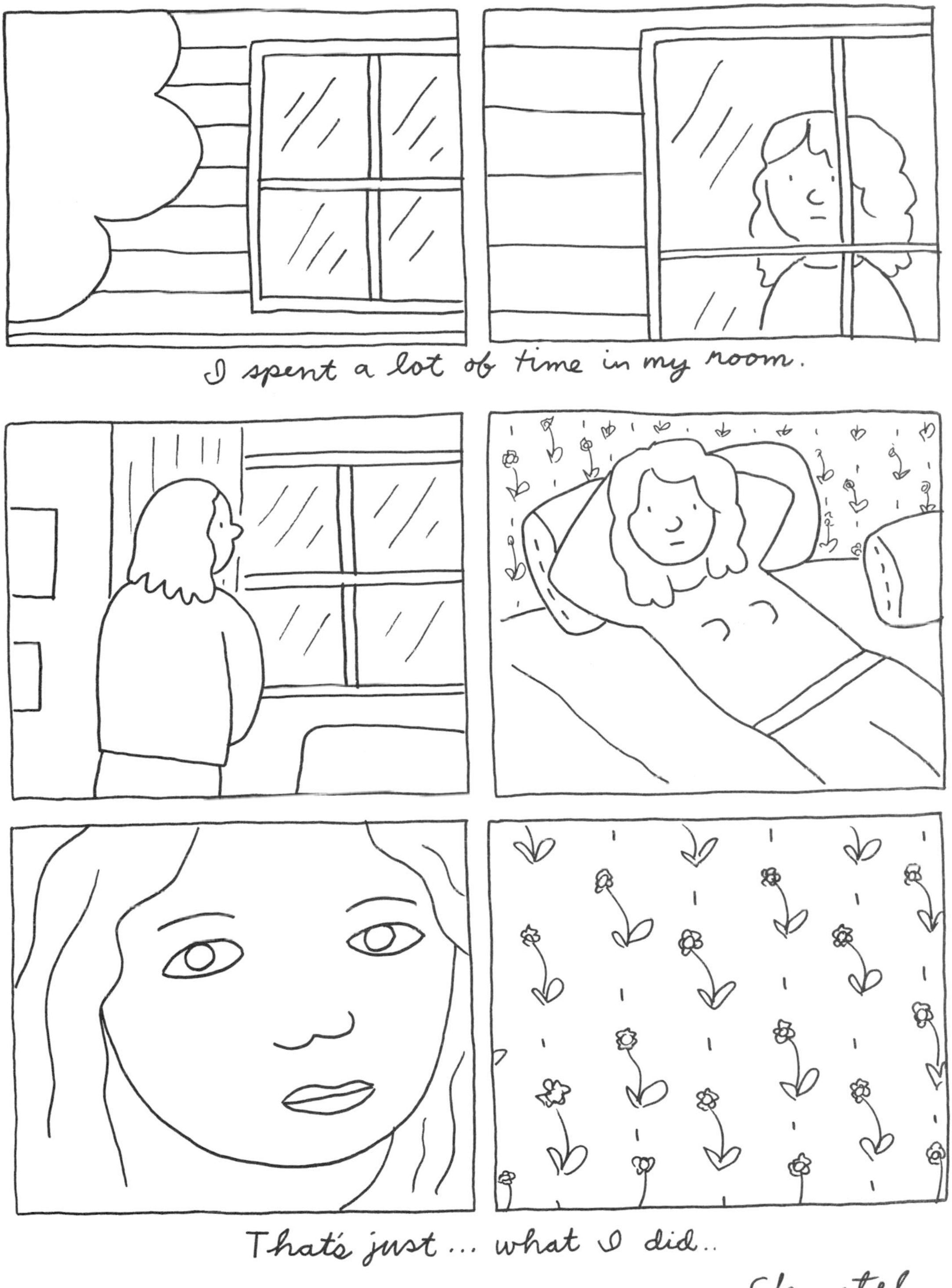
I spent a lot of time in my room.
That's just ... what I did..
Chantel

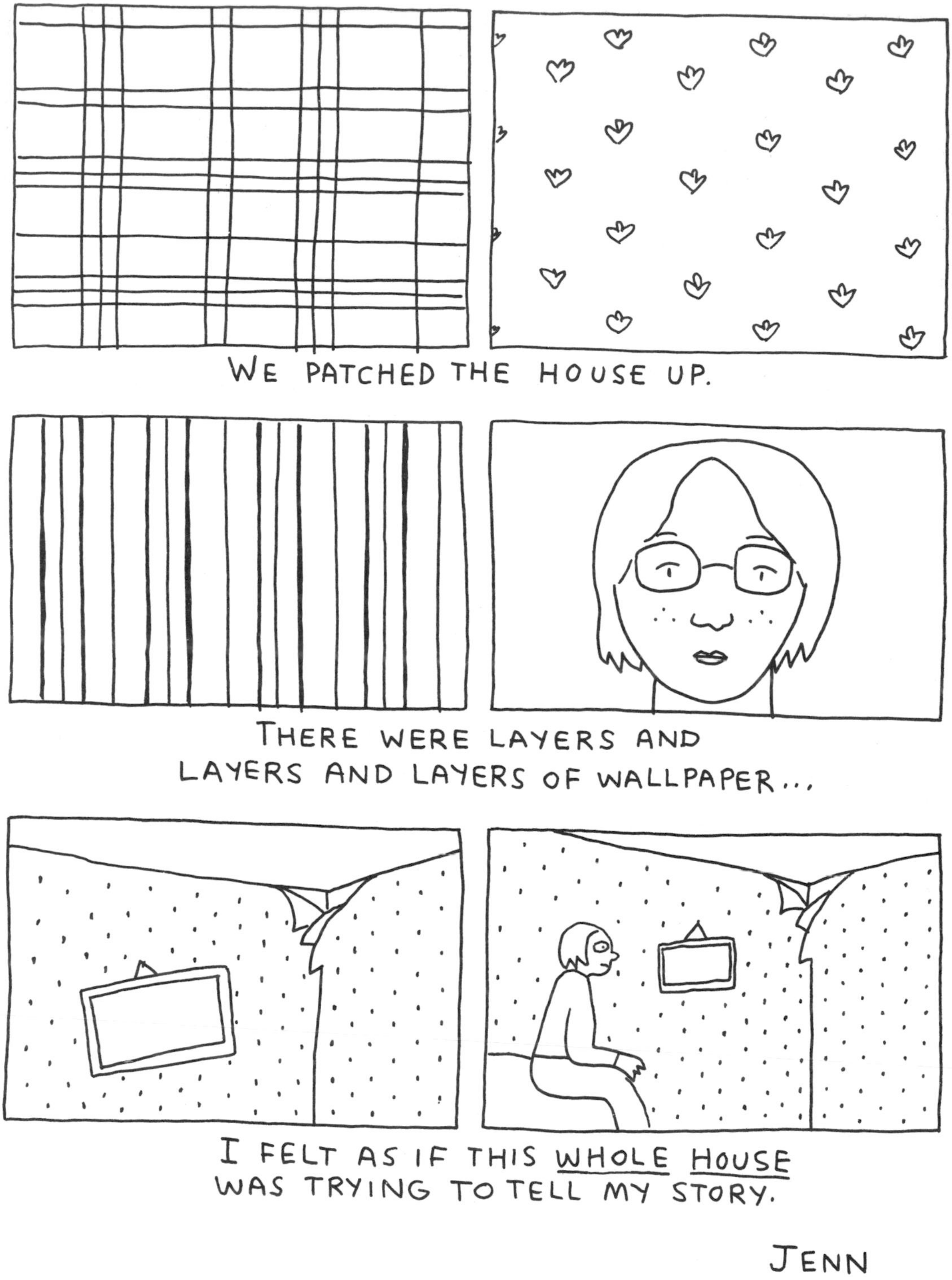
WE PATCHED THE HOUSE UP.
THERE WERE LAYERS AND LAYERS AND LAYERS OF WALLPAPER...
I FELT AS IF THIS WHOLE HOUSE WAS TRYING TO TELL MY STORY.
JENN

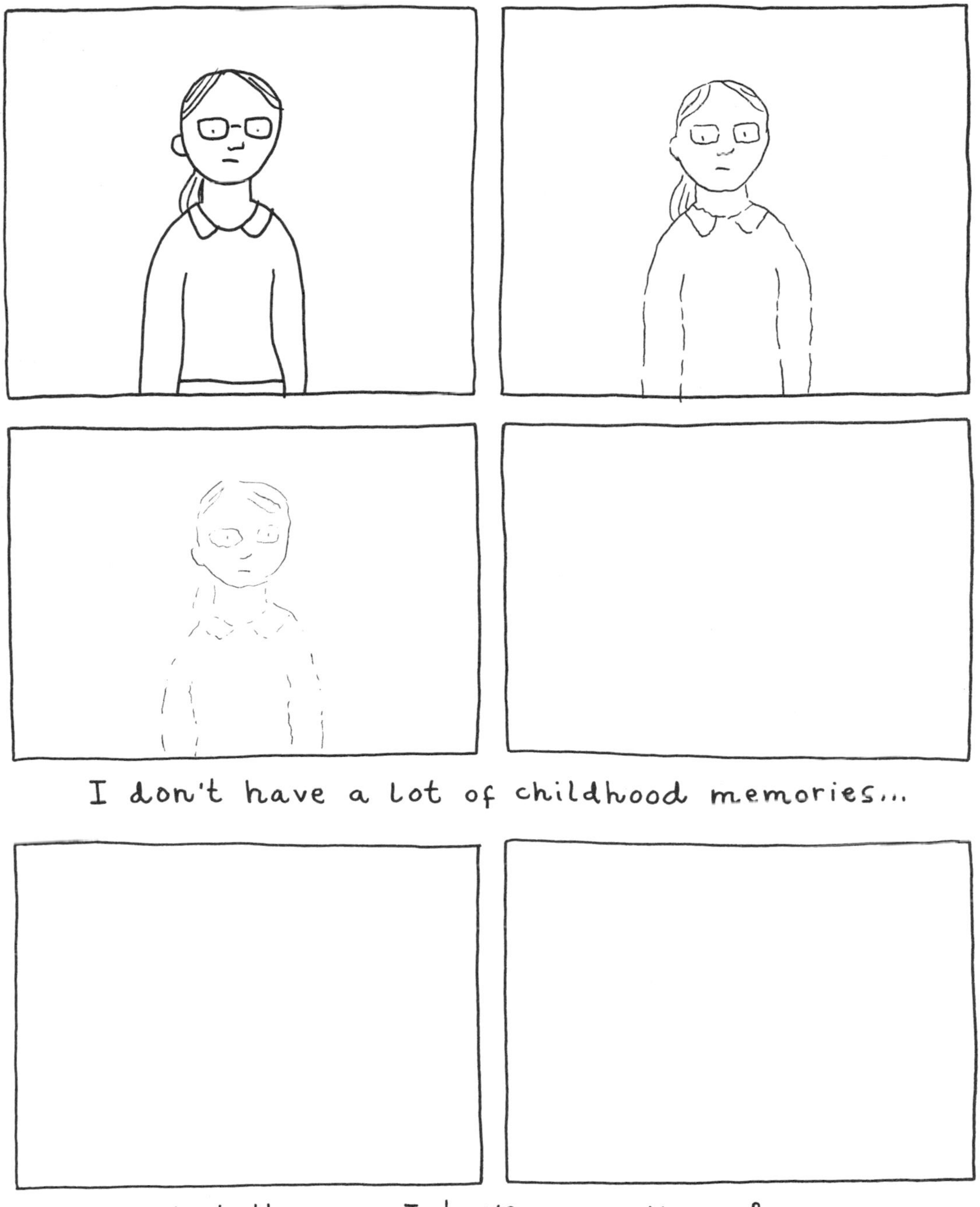
I don't have a lot of childhood memories...
...but the ones I have are all good...

Tina

...pretty much...

Tina

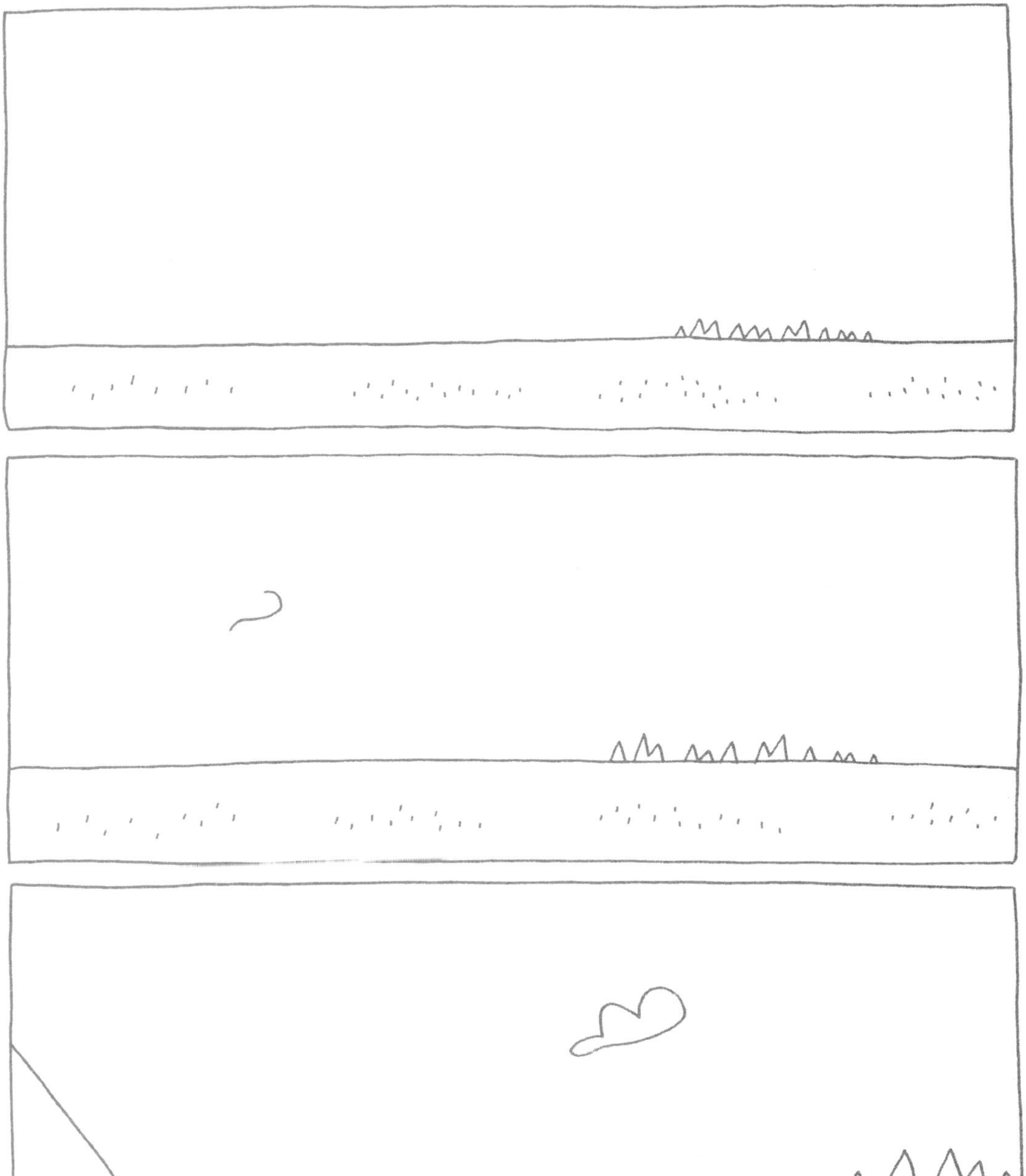

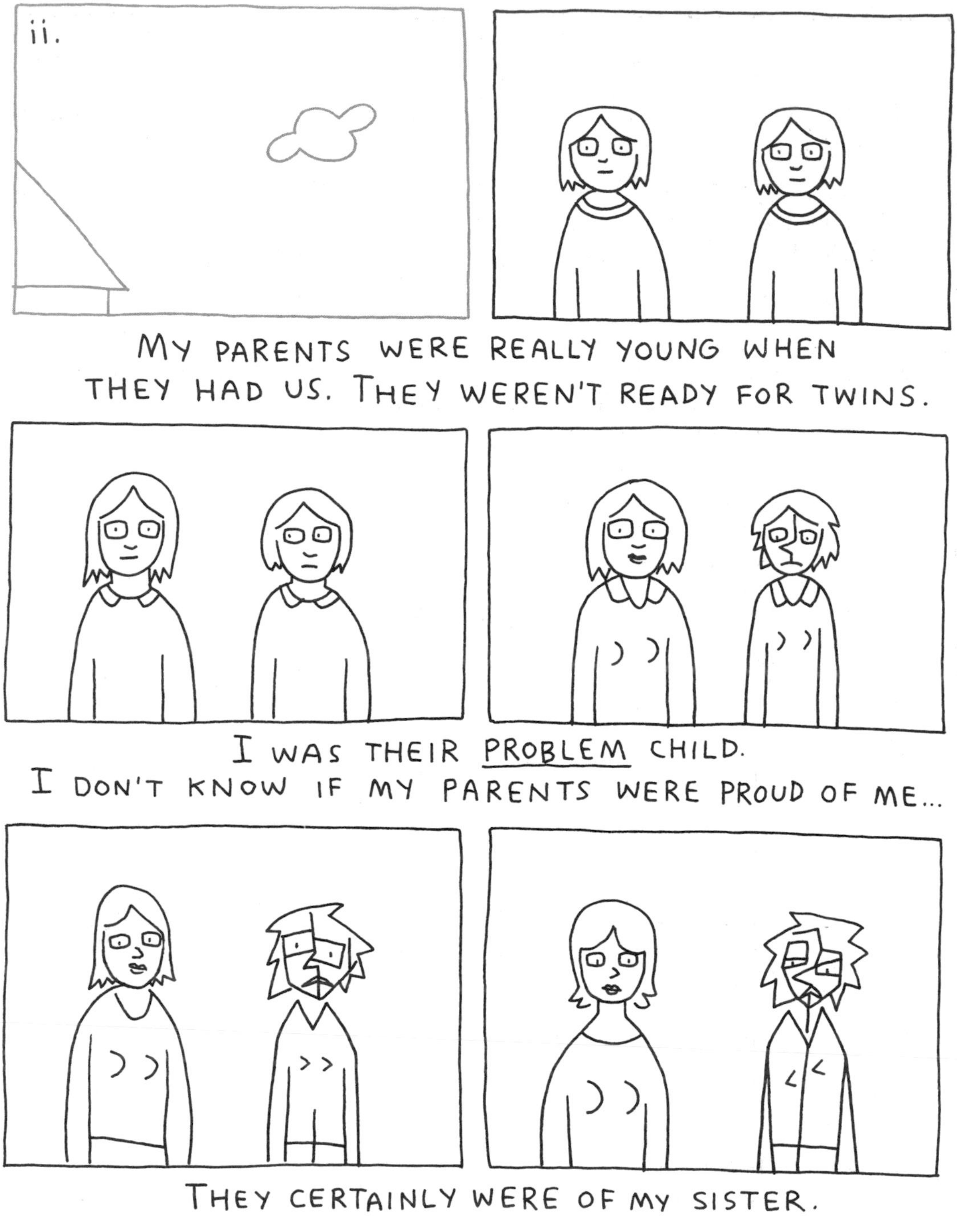
ii.
MY PARENTS WERE REALLY YOUNG WHEN THEY HAD US. THEY WEREN'T READY FOR TWINS.
I WAS THEIR PROBLEM CHILD.
I DON'T KNOW IF MY PARENTS WERE PROUD OF ME...
THEY CERTAINLY WERE OF MY SISTER.

JENN

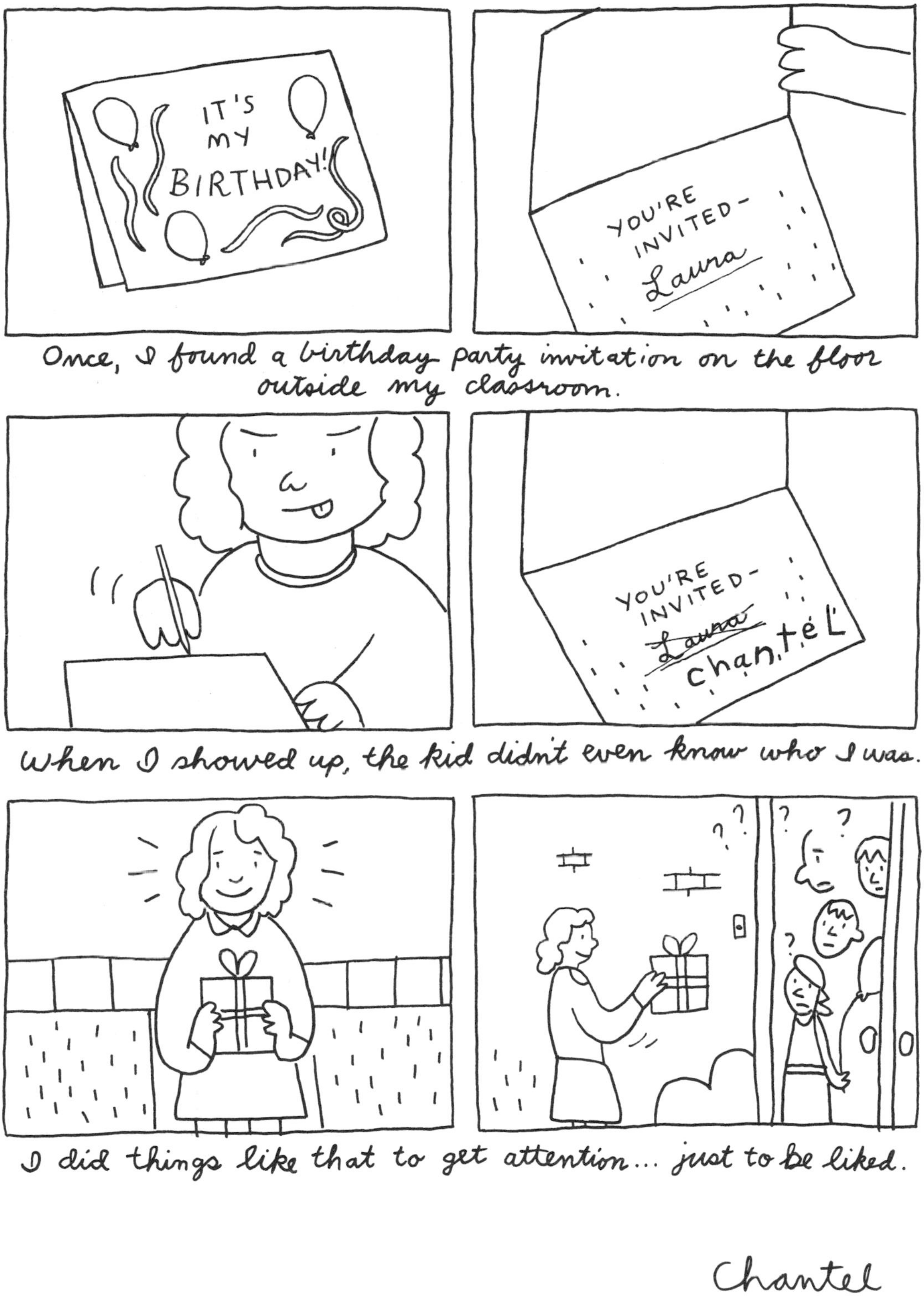
IT'S MY BIRTHDAY!
YOU'RE INVITED- Laura
Once, I found a birthday party invitation on the floor outside my classroom.
YOU'RE INVITED- Laura chanteL
When I showed up, the kid didn't even know who I was.
?
?
?
?
?
I did things like that to get attention… just to be liked.
Chantel

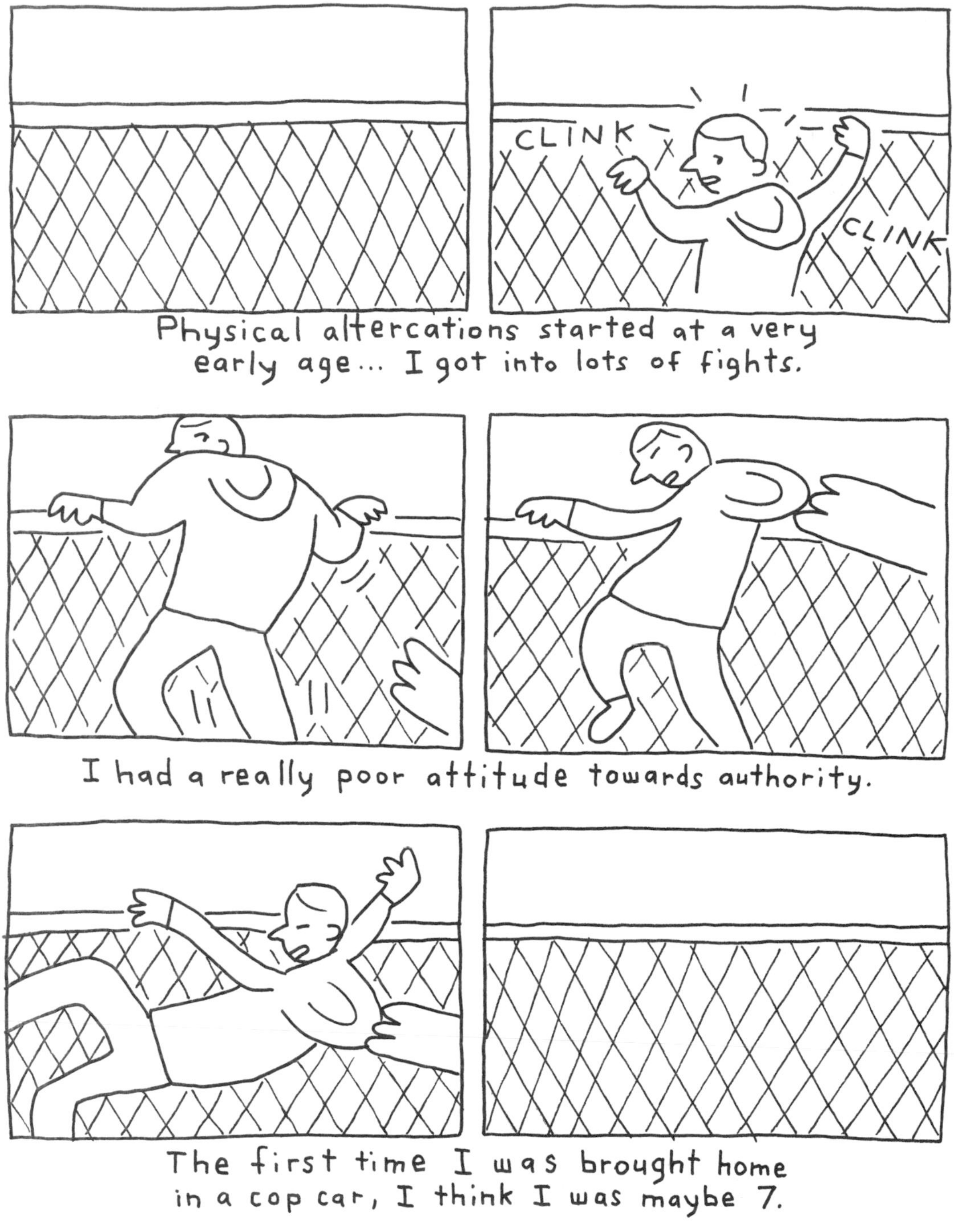
CLINK
CLINK
Physical altercations started at a very early age... I got into lots of fights.
I had a really poor attitude towards authority.
The first time I was brought home in a cop car, I think I was maybe 7.

Ryan

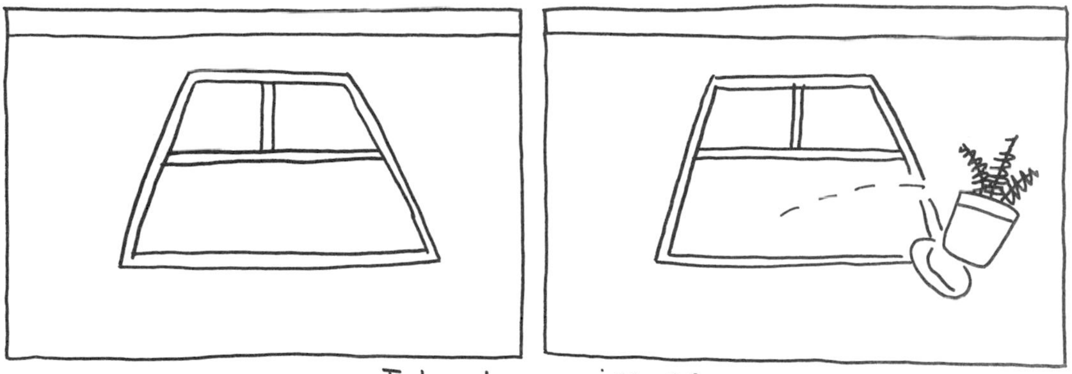

I had rage issues.
I would just fly off the handle for stupid things.

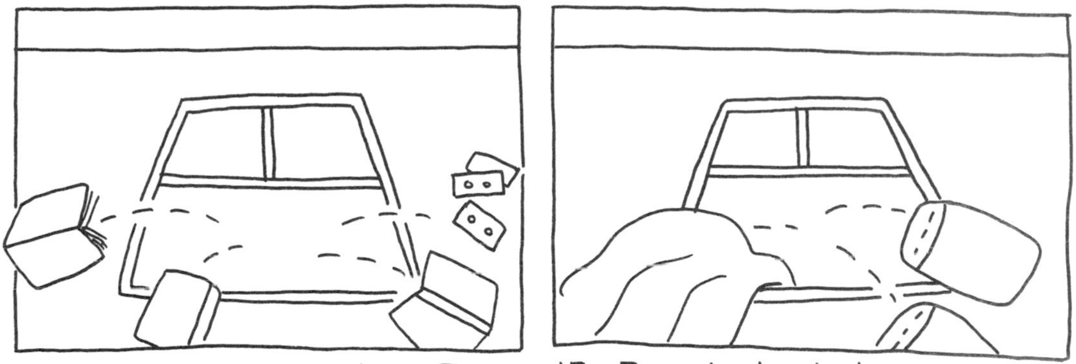

Once when I was 15, I just started
throwing everything out my bedroom window.

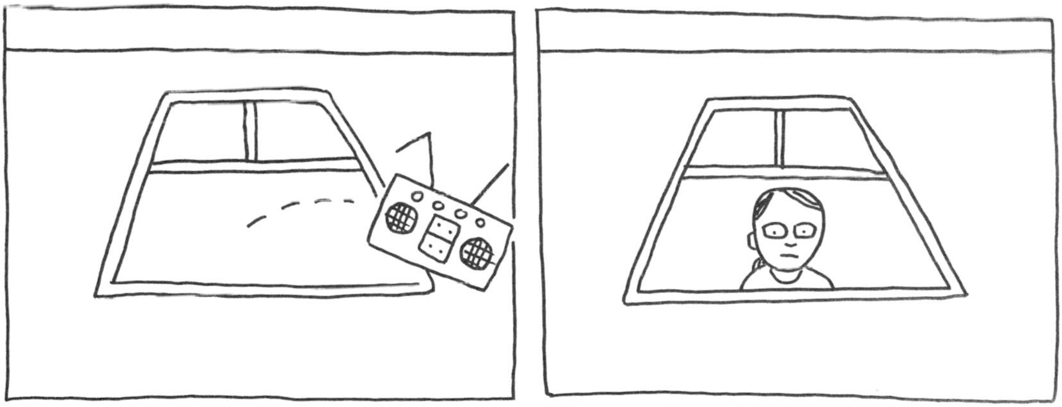

I didn't even know why I was doing it.

Tina

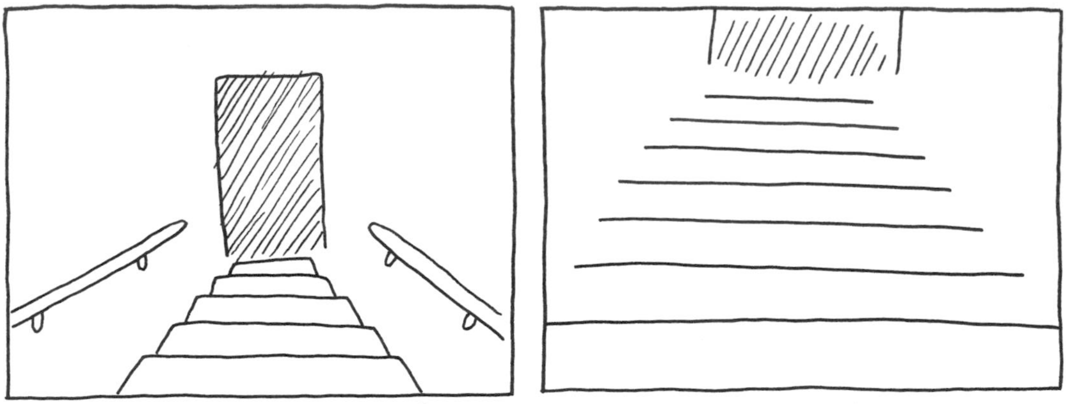

I even threw myself down the stairs a few times.

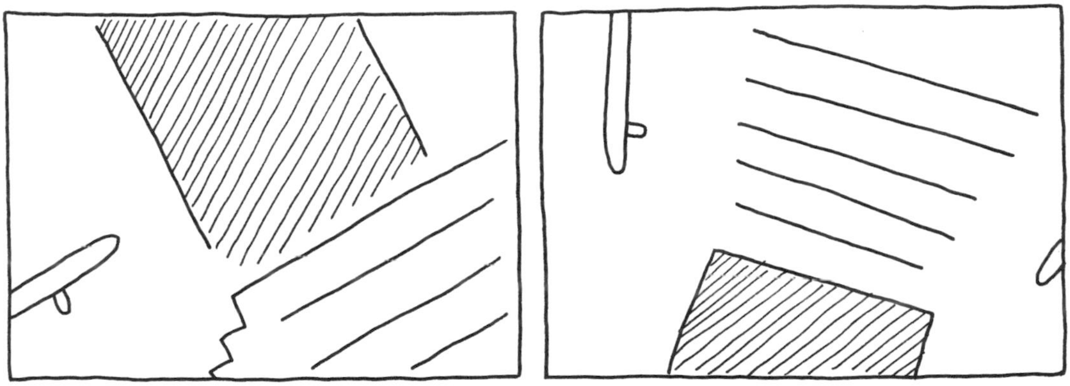

I just really wanted to hurt myself.

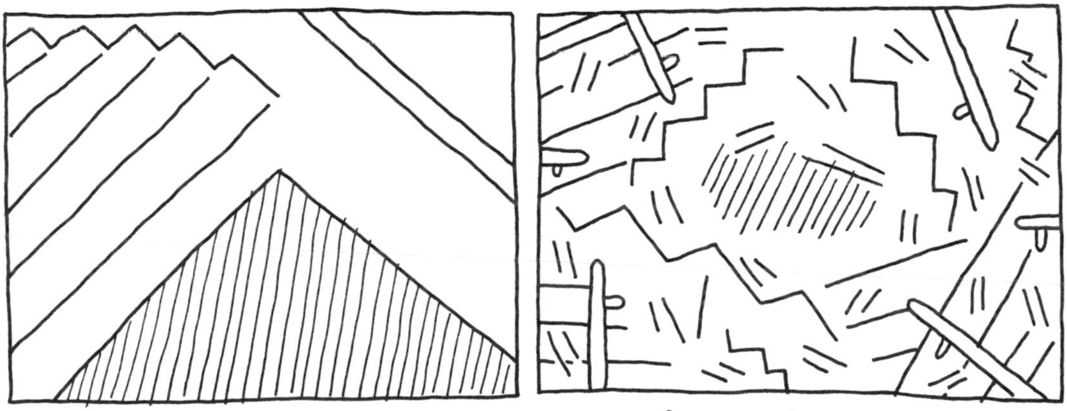

To feel pain is better than to feel nothing...

Tina

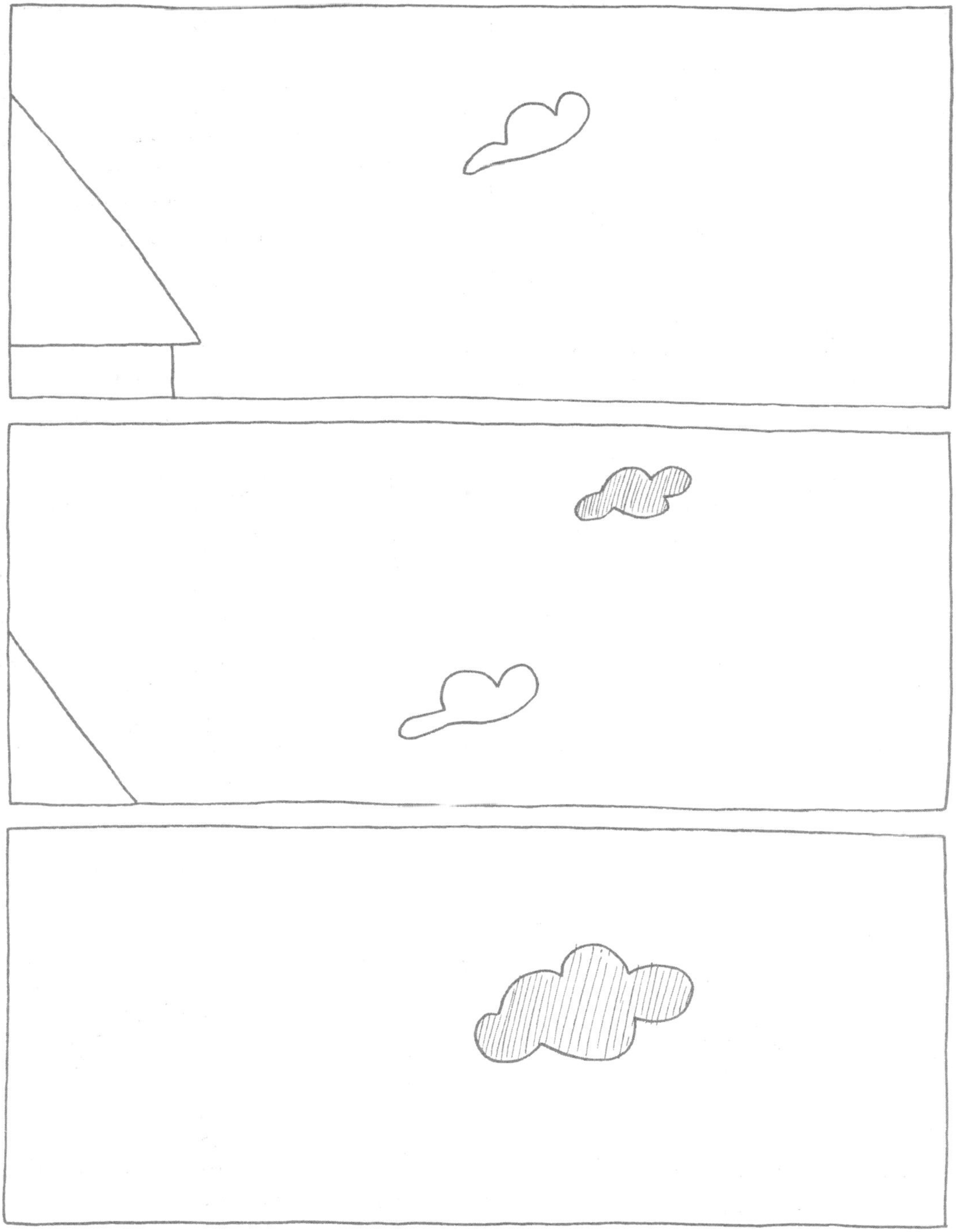

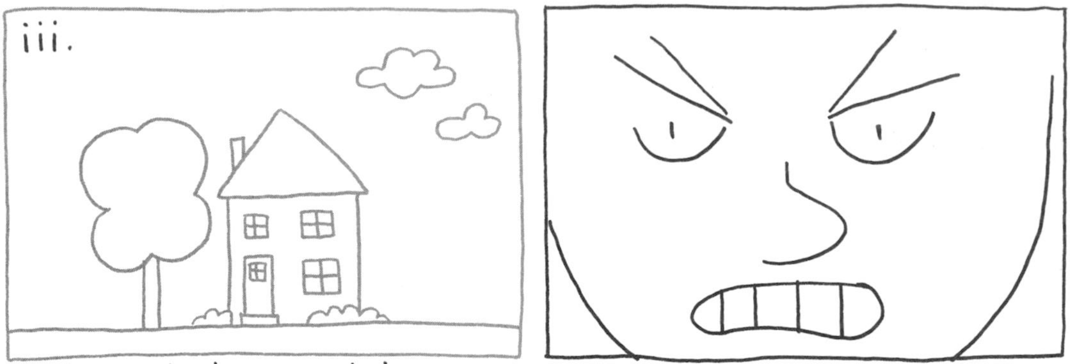
iii.

I believe a lot of people with mental disorders or addiction problems come from broken families.

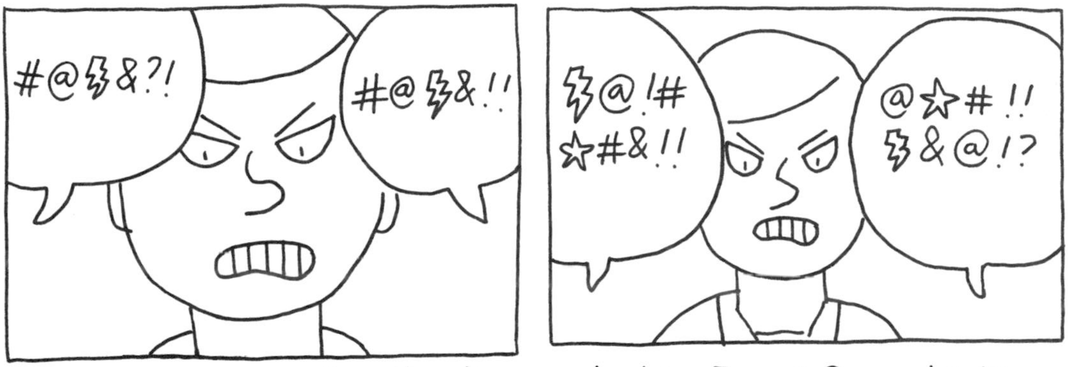

My parents finally divorced when I was 9, maybe 10. My dad was cheating.

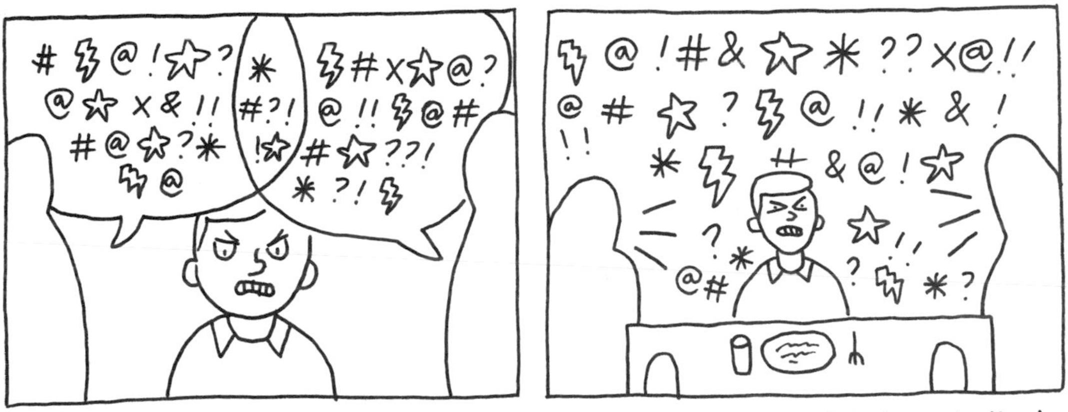

I was angry. I didn't understand... and I completely rebelled.

Ryan

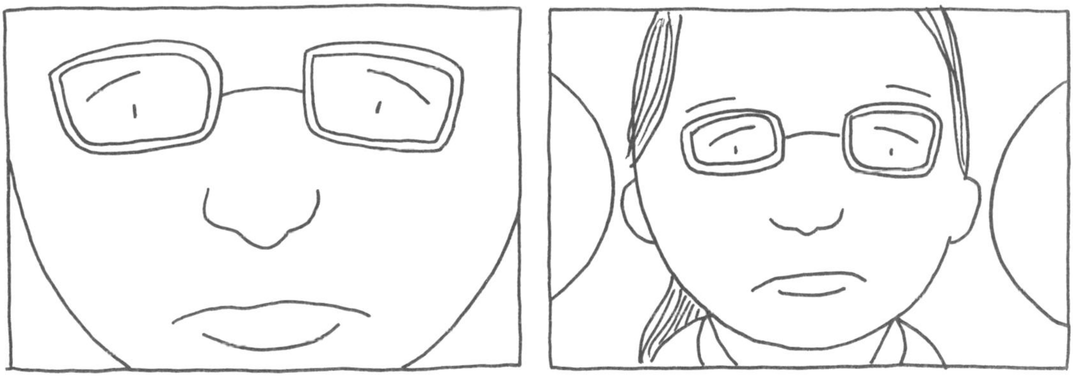

I had the best mom and dad in the world,
but I was just never happy.

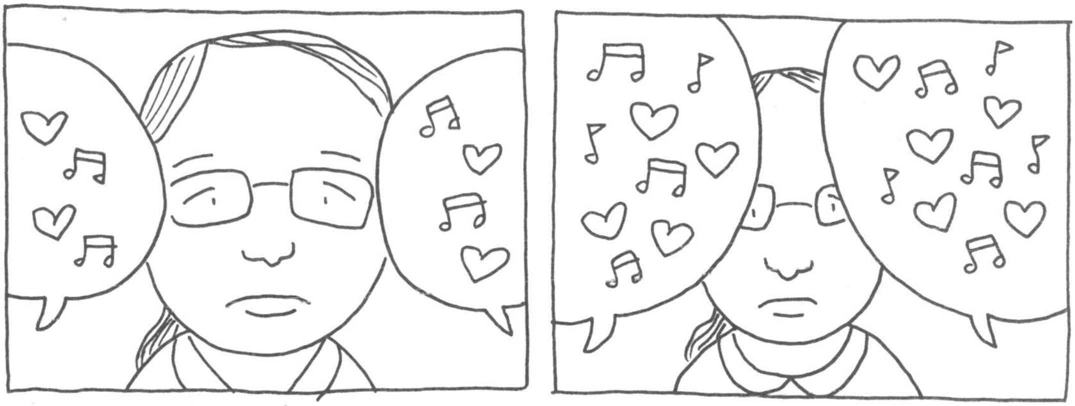

My parents didn't know there was anything <u>wrong</u> with me...

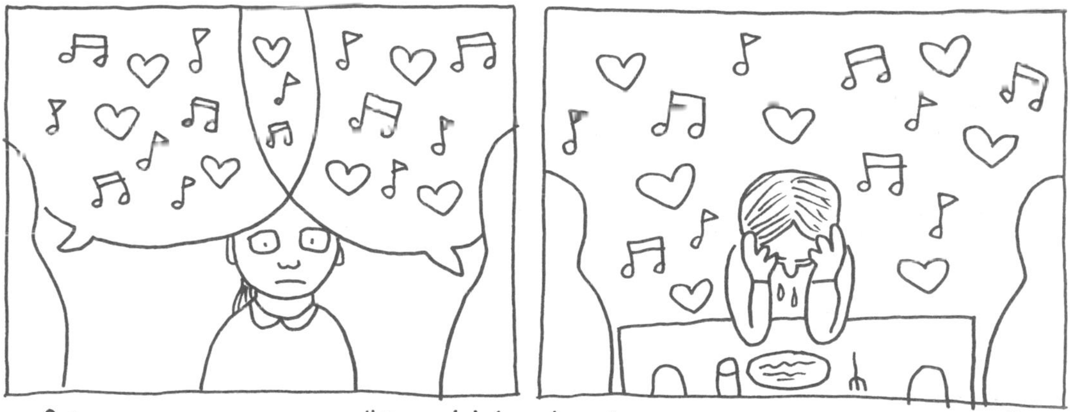

As my mom says, "You kids don't come with manuals."

Tina

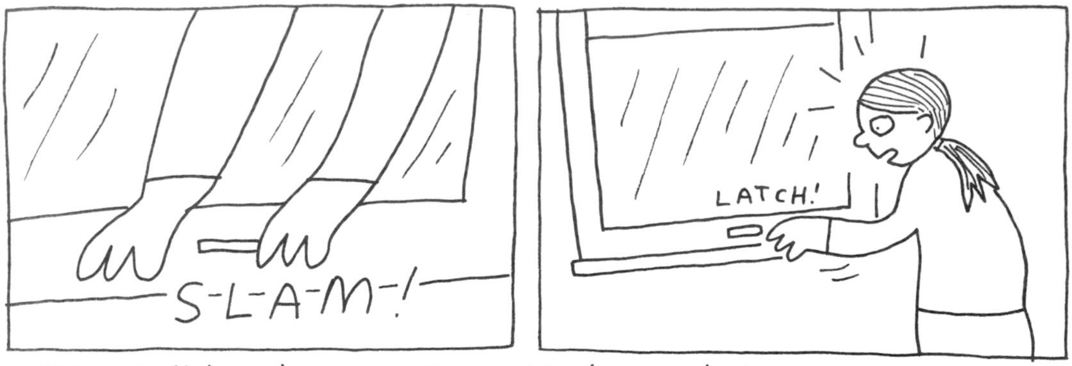
S-L-A-M-!
LATCH!

I had this strange fear that somebody was going to break into the house and do something to me.

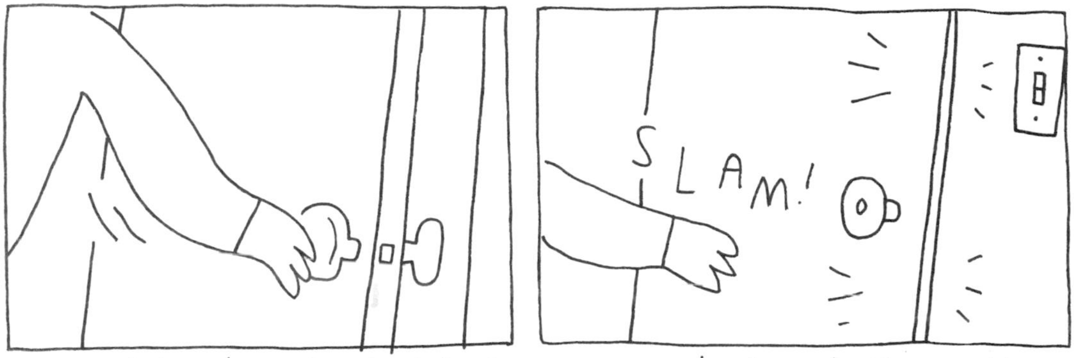
SLAM!

I used to sleep tucked between my bed and the wall. Sometimes I slept in the closet.

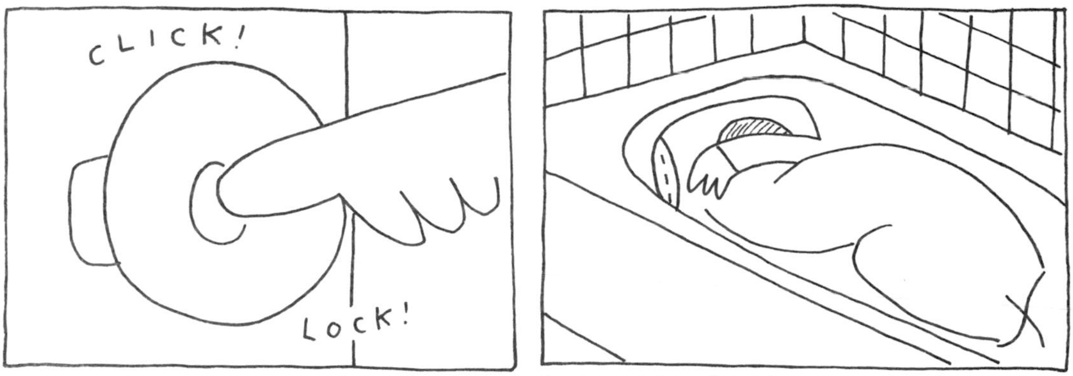
CLICK!
LOCK!

Once I slept in the bathtub. The bathroom door was the only one with a lock on it.

Tina

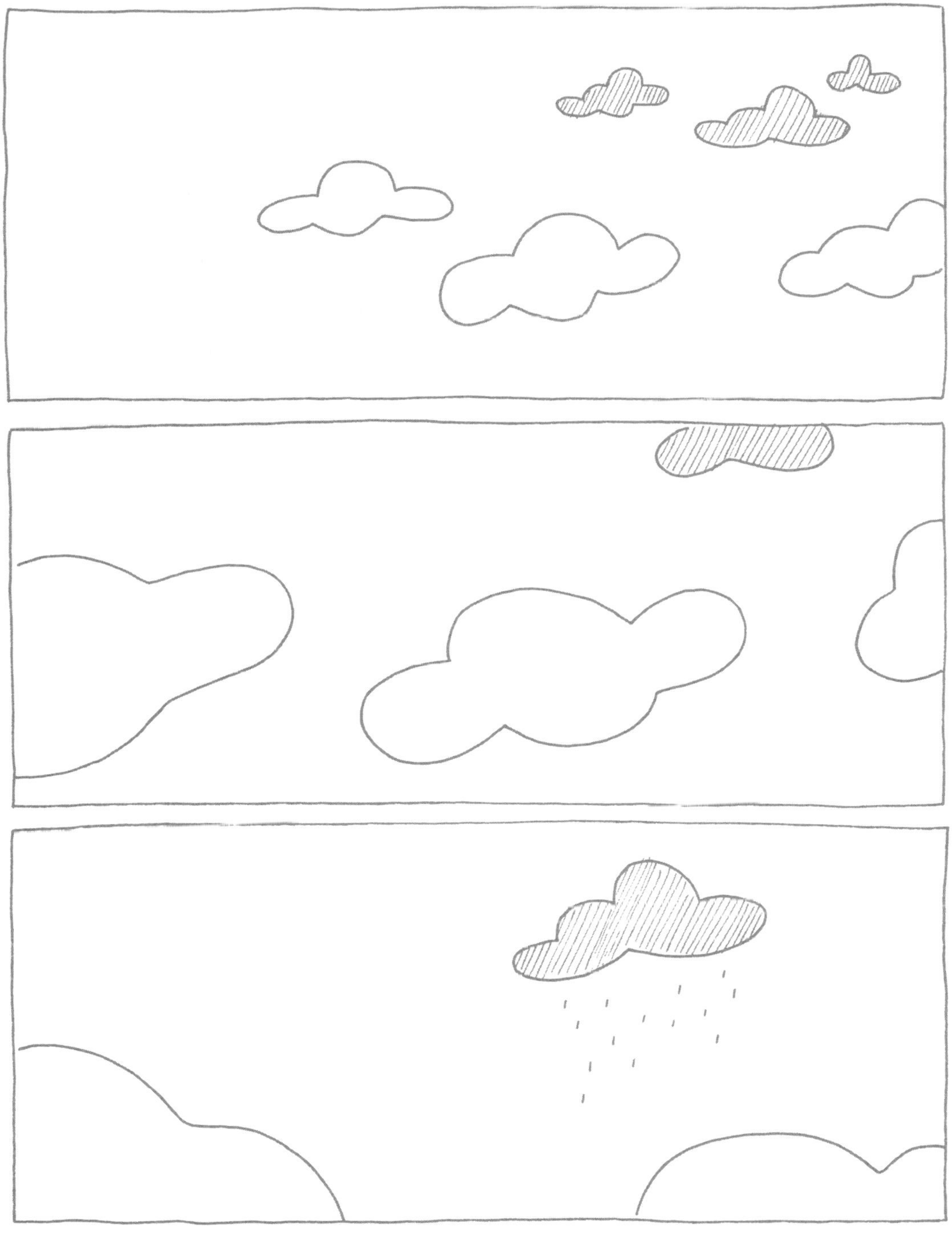

iv.

EVEN AT 9, I DIDN'T WANT TO BE ALIVE.

I THINK THAT'S PART OF WHERE THE
EATING DISORDER CAME IN.

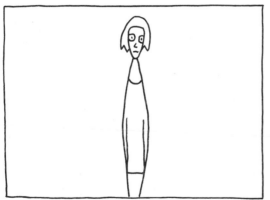

I COULD AT LEAST SLOWLY FADE AWAY...

JENN

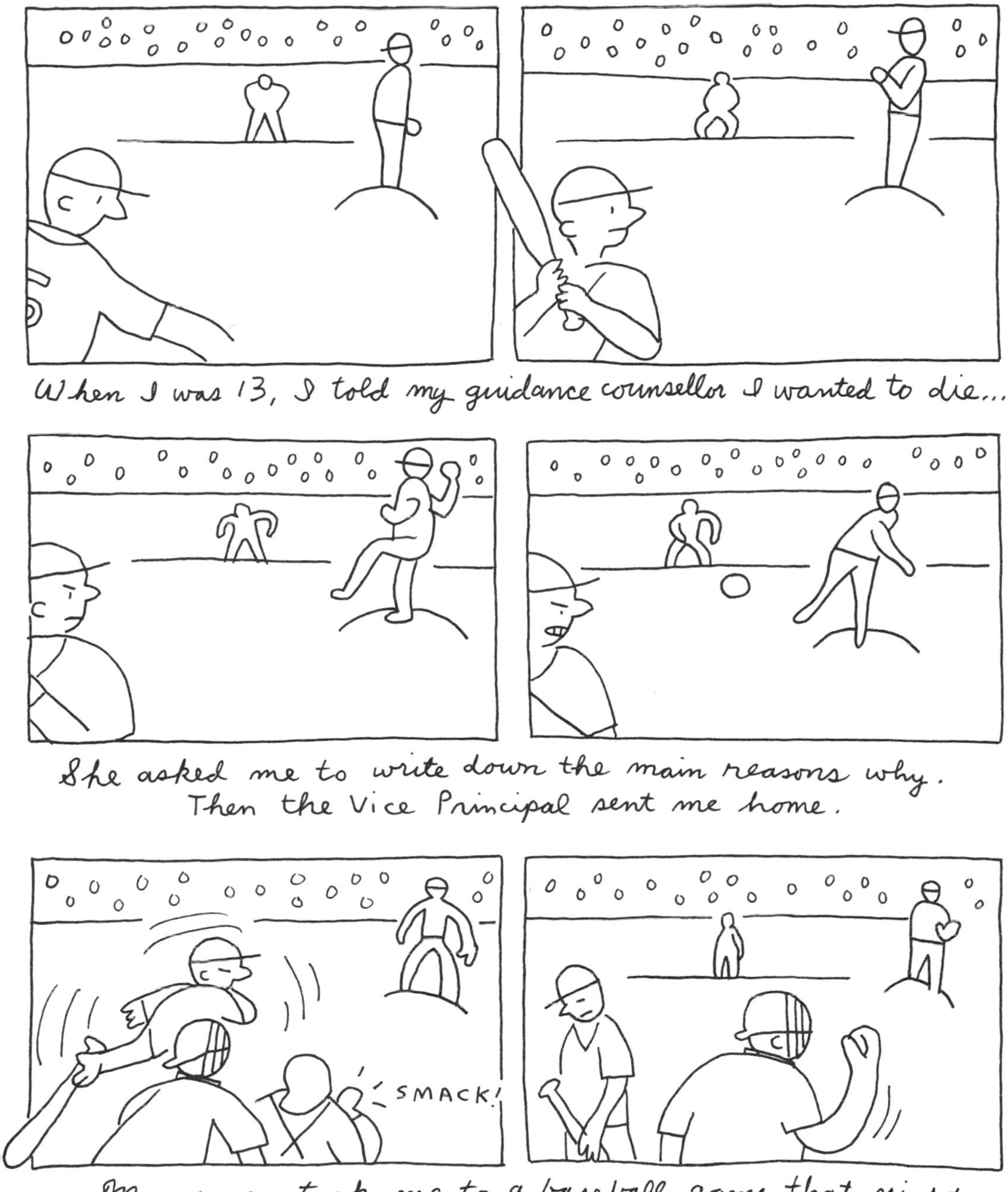
When I was 13, I told my guidance counsellor I wanted to die...
She asked me to write down the main reasons why.
Then the Vice Principal sent me home.
SMACK!
My mom took me to a baseball game that night...
just to try and fix it.

Chantel

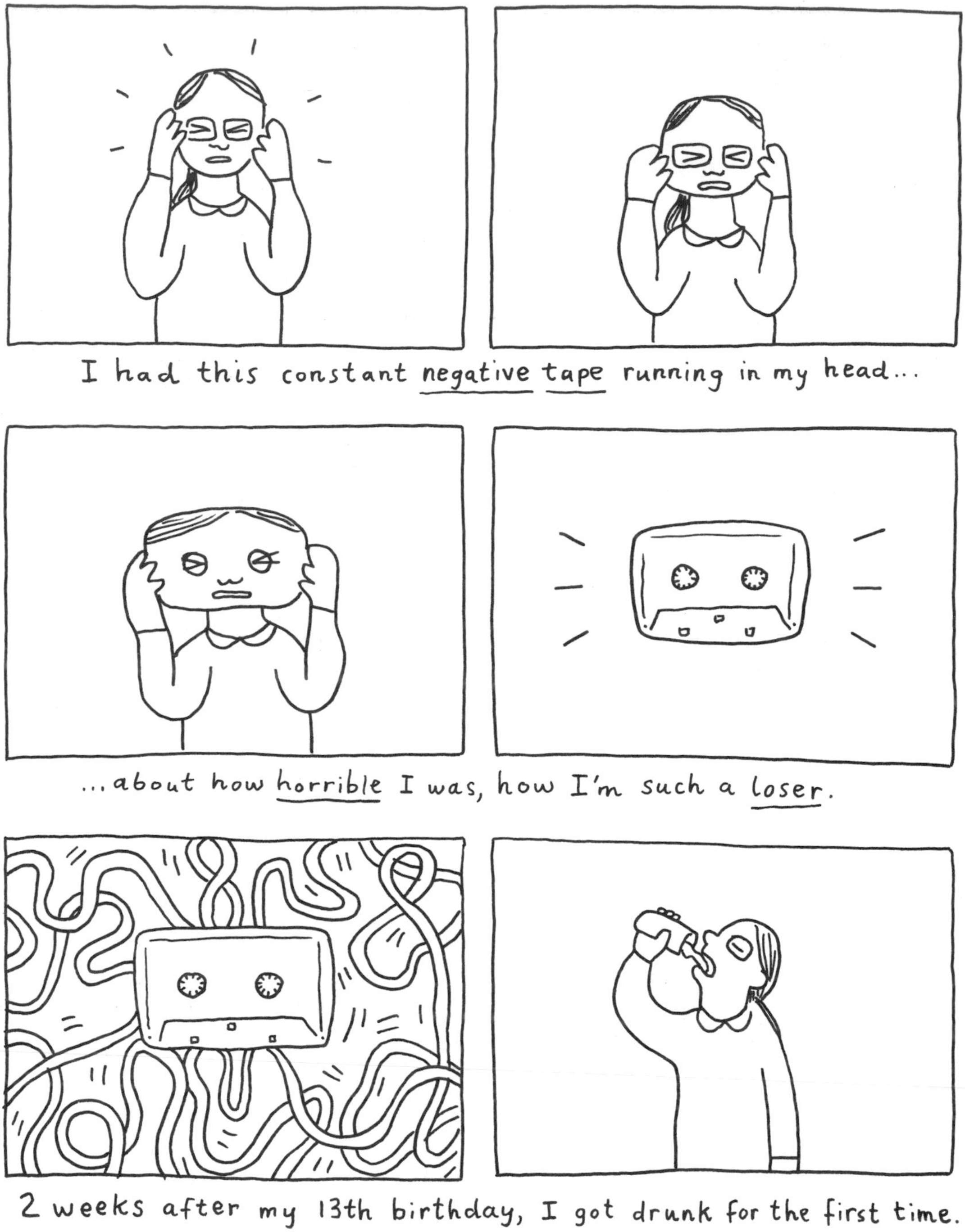
I had this constant negative tape running in my head...
...about how horrible I was, how I'm such a loser.
2 weeks after my 13th birthday, I got drunk for the first time.

Tina

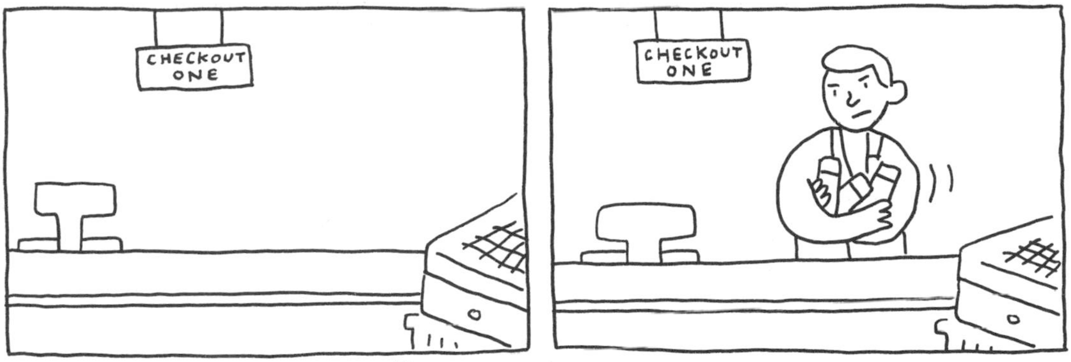
CHECKOUT ONE
CHECKOUT ONE

At 12, I was out of control. I was using <u>inhalants</u> to the point where I was almost committed to hospital.

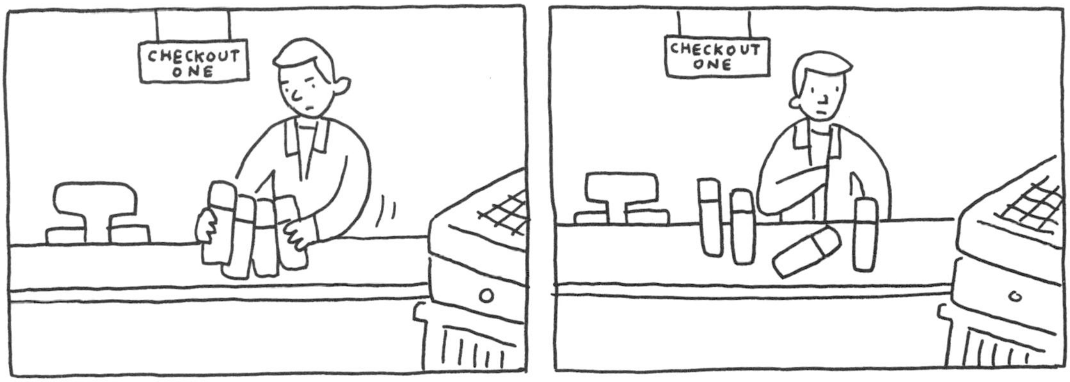
CHECKOUT ONE
CHECKOUT ONE

Then I was diagnosed as bipolar. That was when I was 14.

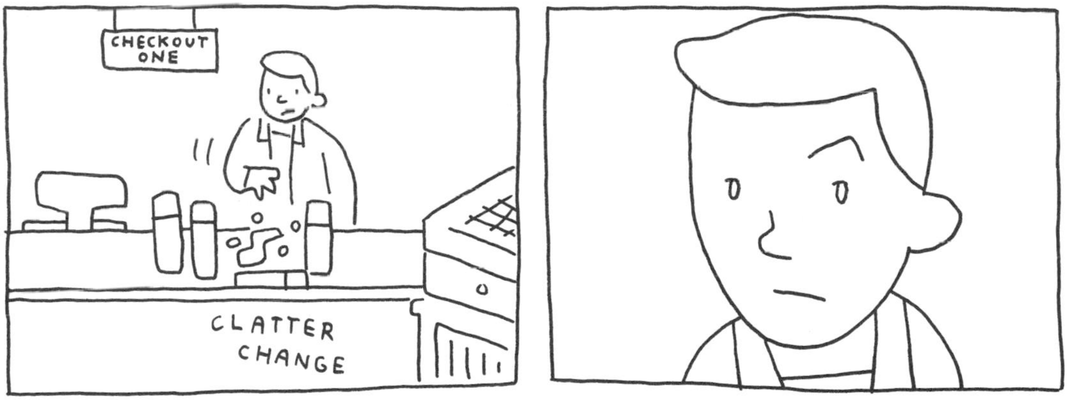
CHECKOUT ONE
CLATTER
CHANGE

There was clearly a much larger problem than just my attitude.

Ryan

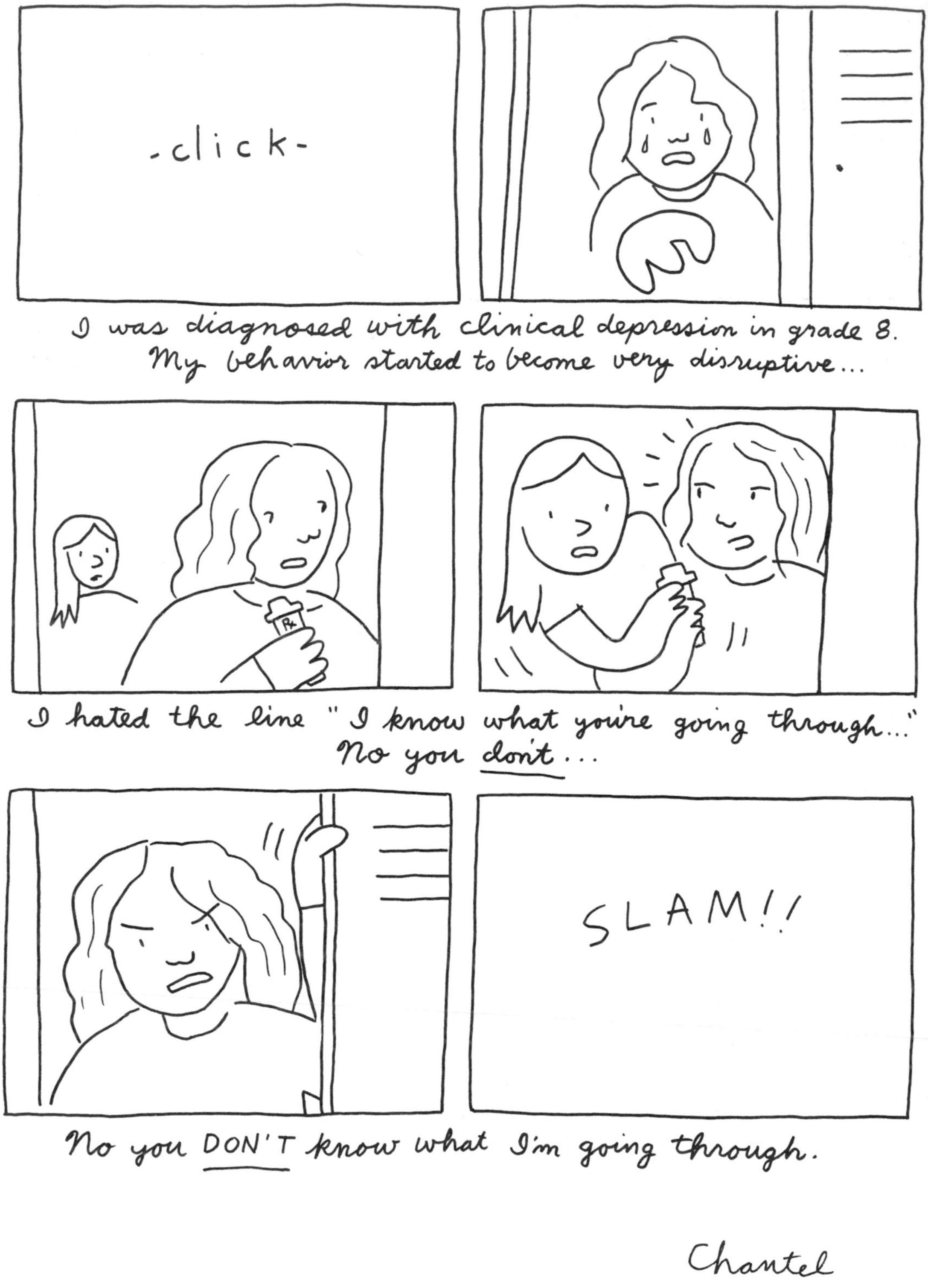
-click-
I was diagnosed with clinical depression in grade 8.
My behavior started to become very disruptive...
I hated the line "I know what you're going through..."
No you don't...
SLAM!!
No you DON'T know what I'm going through.
Chantel

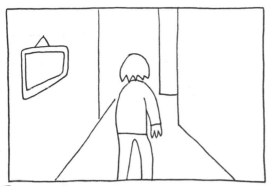

THEY ALWAYS HAD A REASON FOR WHY I WAS SAD. "OH, SHE'S TOO <u>THIN</u>, SHE'S TOO <u>FAT</u>, SHE'S TOO <u>THIS</u>, SHE'S TOO <u>THAT</u>."

"OH, HER <u>PARENTS</u> ARE NEVER HOME. OH, SHE'S JUST A TWIN..."

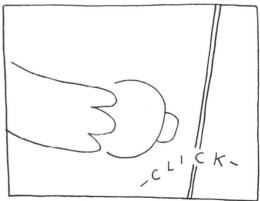

BUT NO ONE EVER <u>ASKED</u>...

JENN

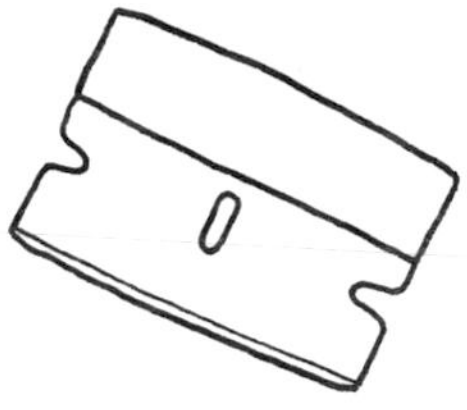

I BECAME A CUTTER.
IT WAS A PAIN I COULD CONTROL.

JENN

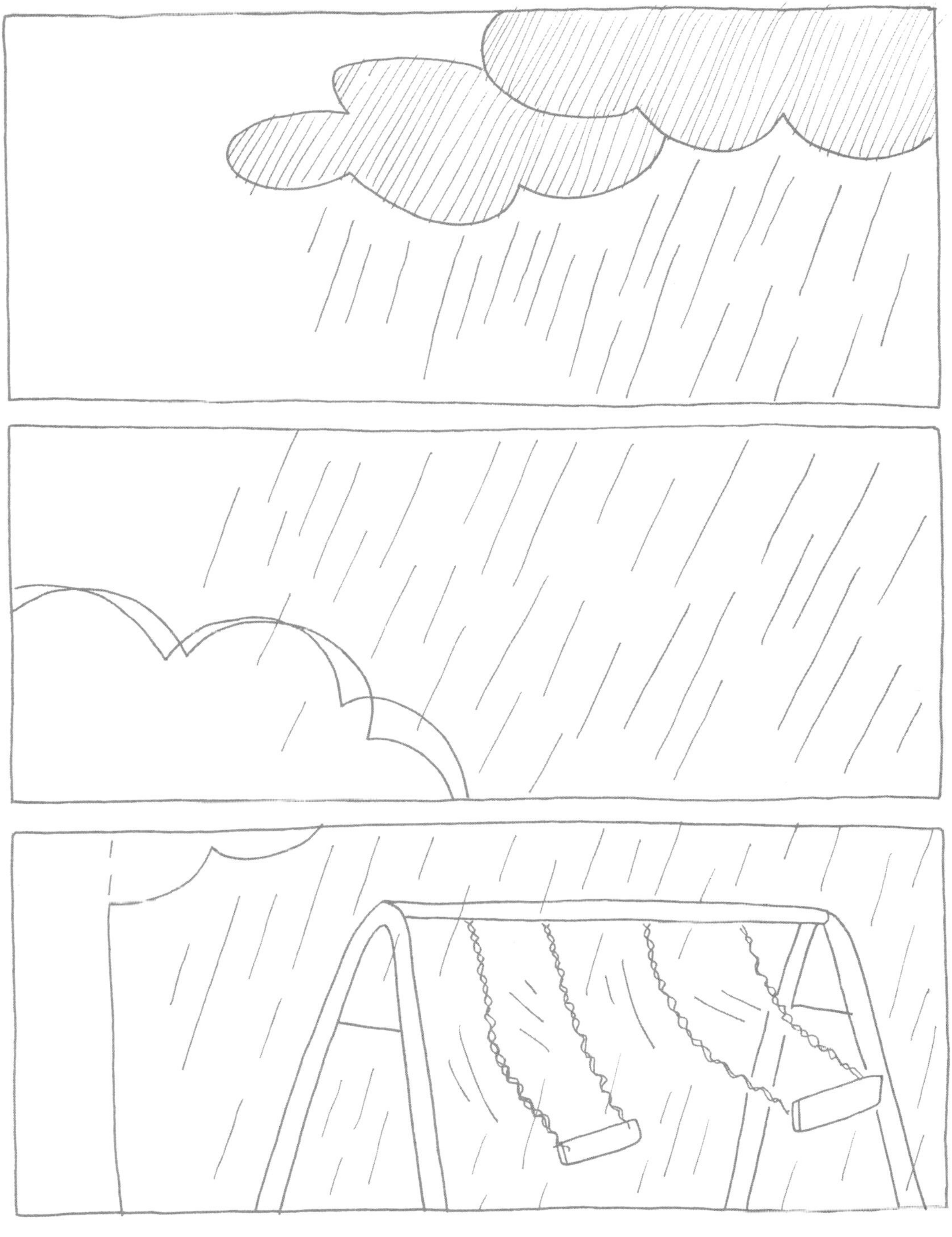

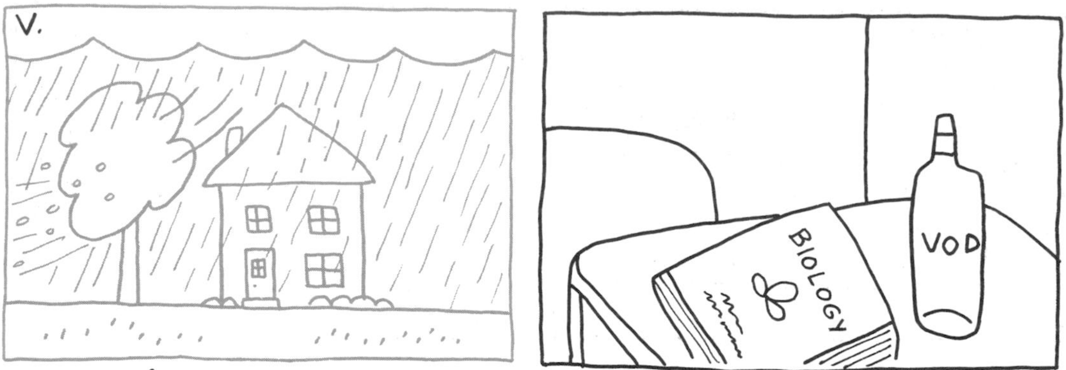
V.
BIOLOGY
VOD

The manic side of my personality came out when I was in high school.

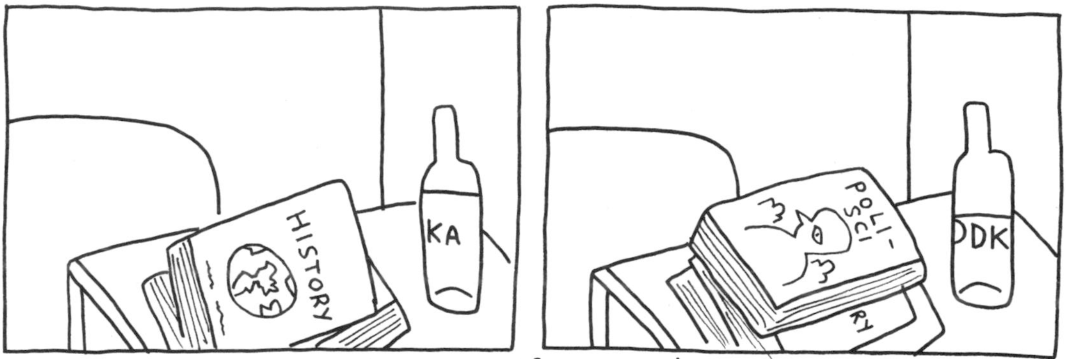
HISTORY
KA
POLI-SCI
ODK

I was doing really well in school... but with that came me drinking...

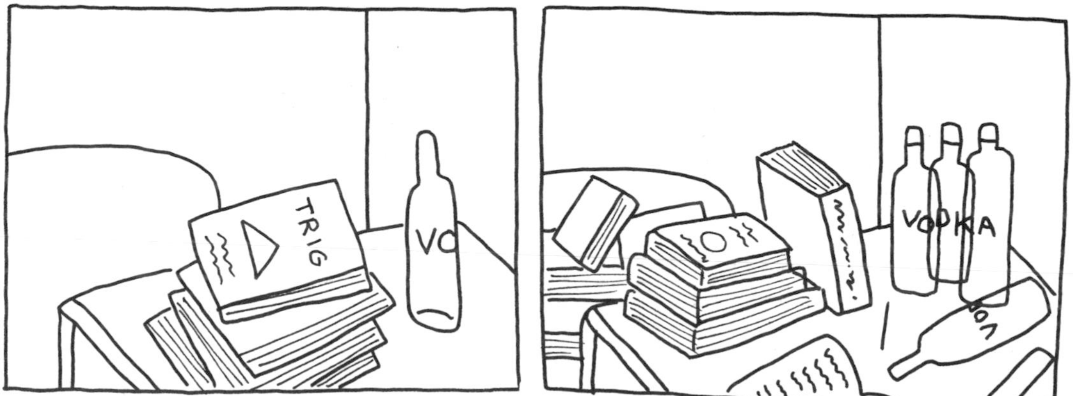
TRIG
VO
VODKA

... a <u>lot</u> ...

Chantel

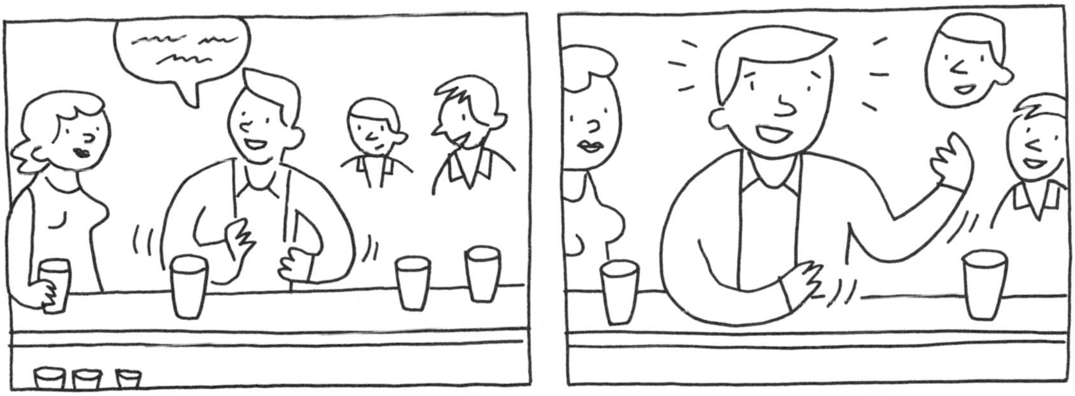

When I'm in my manic phase, I am larger than life.

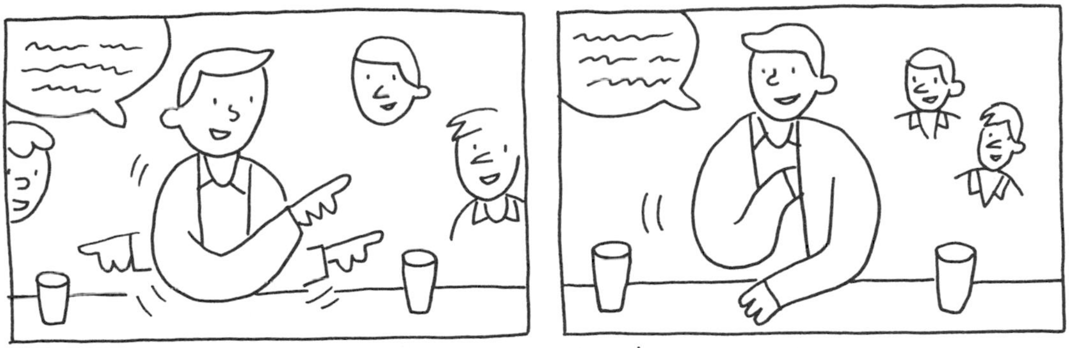

I spend money ridiculously, and I lie...
I lie about who I am, what I do, where I'm at.

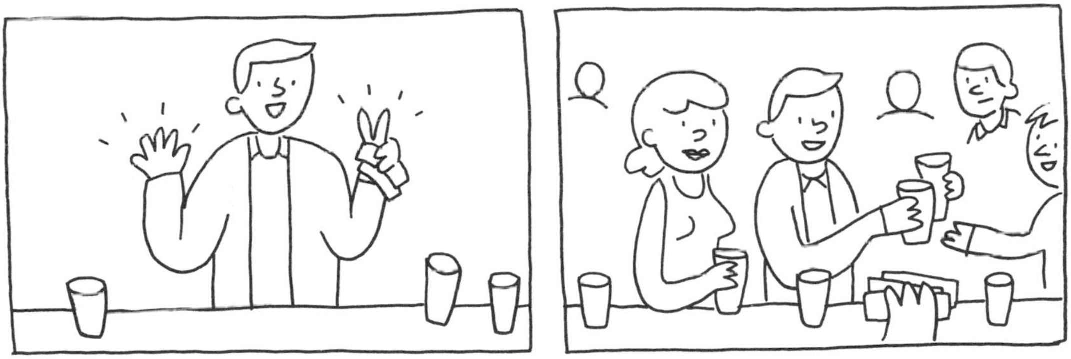

Out in the real world, people don't believe you...
but you believe every word you're saying.

Ryan

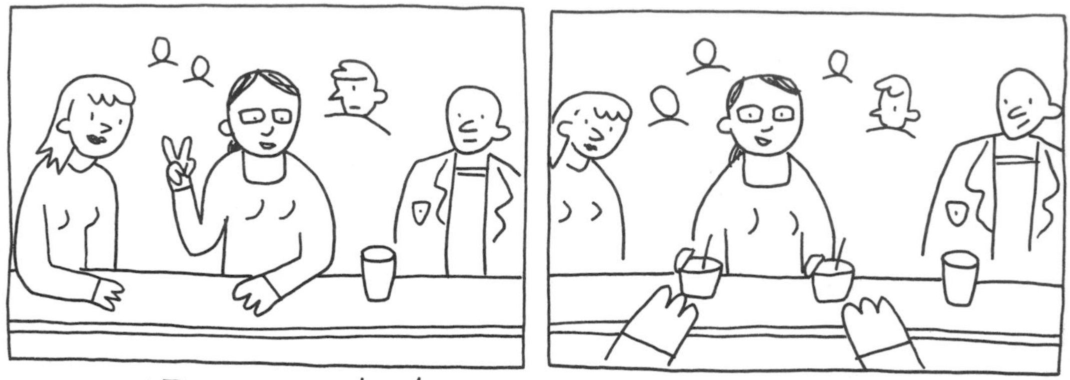

17 was a bad age for me, because I found out I could get served at bars.

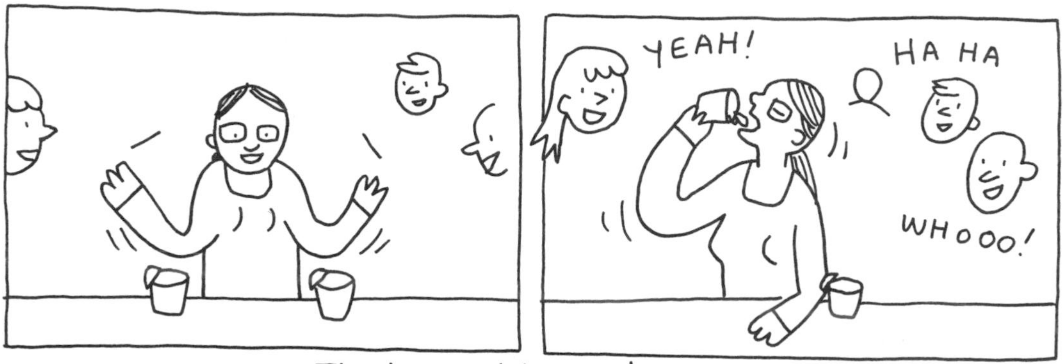
YEAH!
HA HA
WHOOO!

That was like a drug.
4 days a week I just drank until I blacked out.

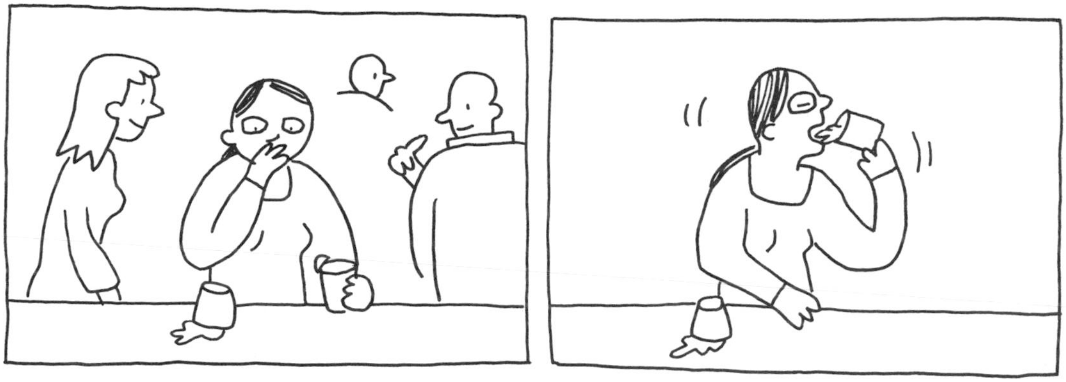

It was an escape...
and it turned off the negative tape in my head.

Tina

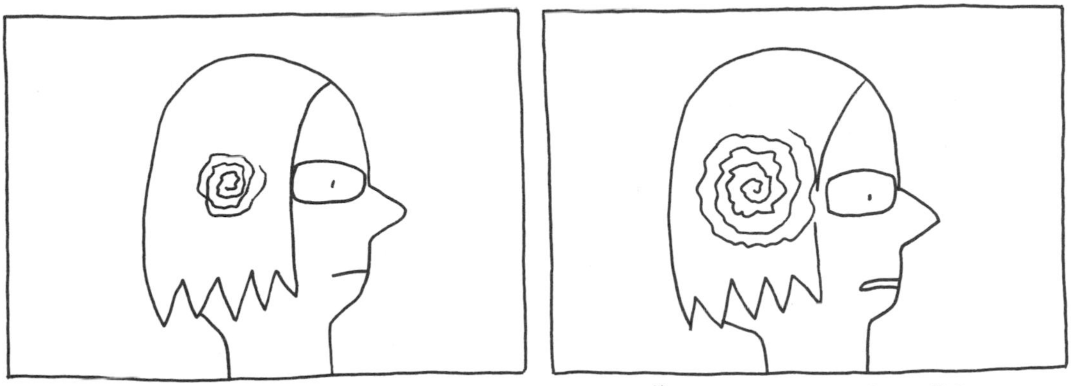

MY THOUGHTS KEPT REPEATING, "YOU'RE WORTHLESS, YOU'VE WRECKED YOUR FAMILY, YOU'RE BROKEN..."

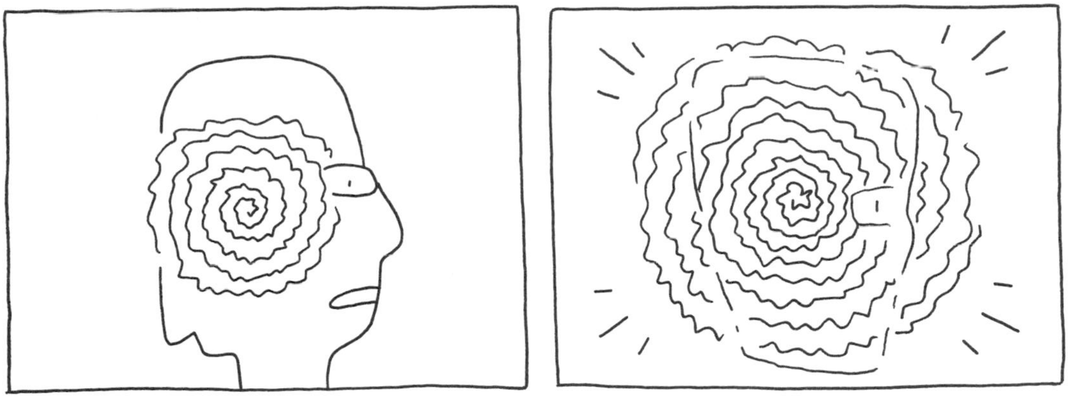

I MEAN, IF YOU BREAK A GLASS, YOU THROW IT OUT.

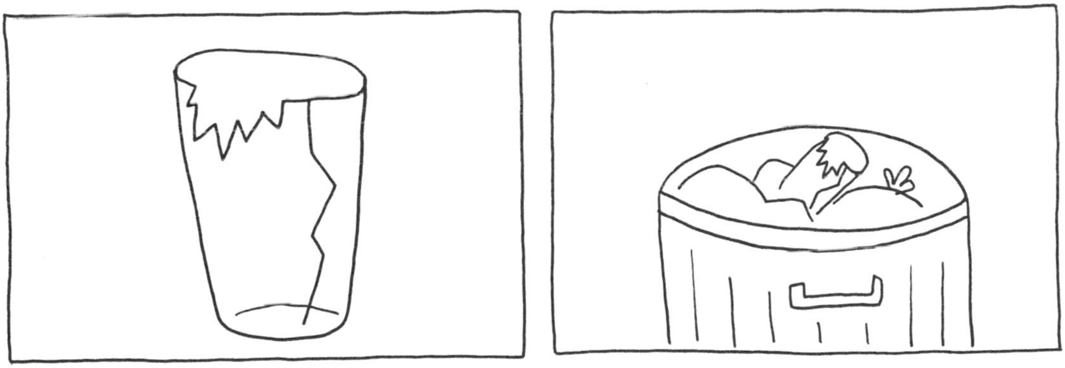

WHO WOULD EVER WANT SOMEONE WHO'S BEEN PLAYED WITH BY SOMEONE ELSE FOR 12 YEARS?

JENN

There are days where I go really really fast. I'm talking really really fast. My thoughts are really really fast.

I feel like I'm yelling in my head. I feel like I'm going "blaaaaaaahh!" really really loud. Like I'm just singing in my head, and I can't understand anything.

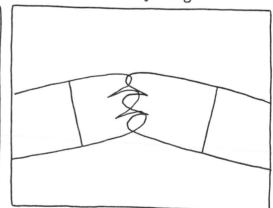

That's usually when I get into a relationship.

Chantel

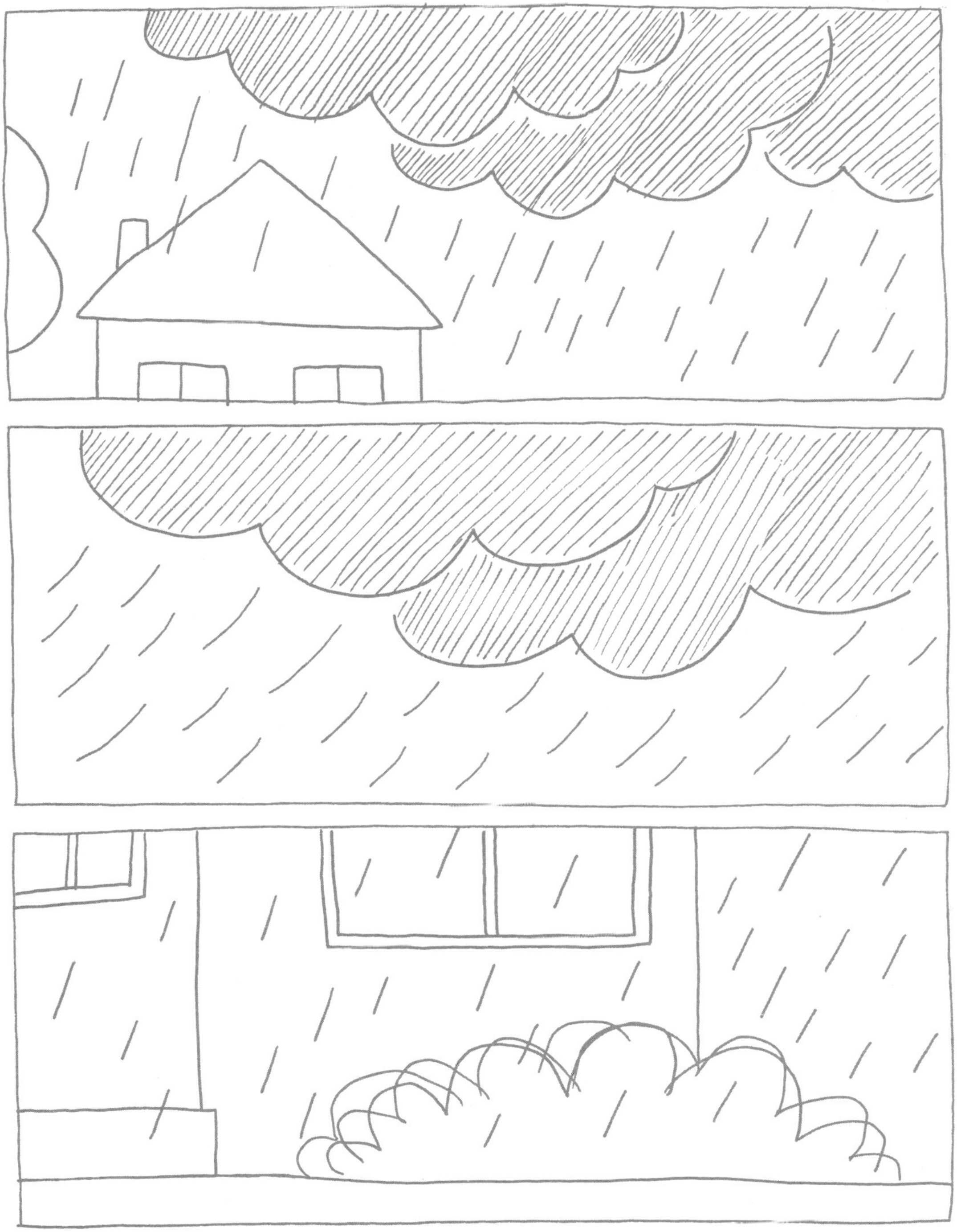

In my first year of university
I got involved with 2 married men.

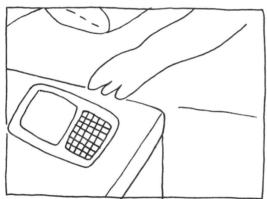

Because I'm _broken_, I can't give 100% of myself to anyone...

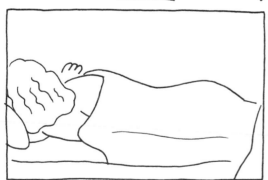

So it's easier to be with someone
who can't give 100% of himself to _me_.

Chantel

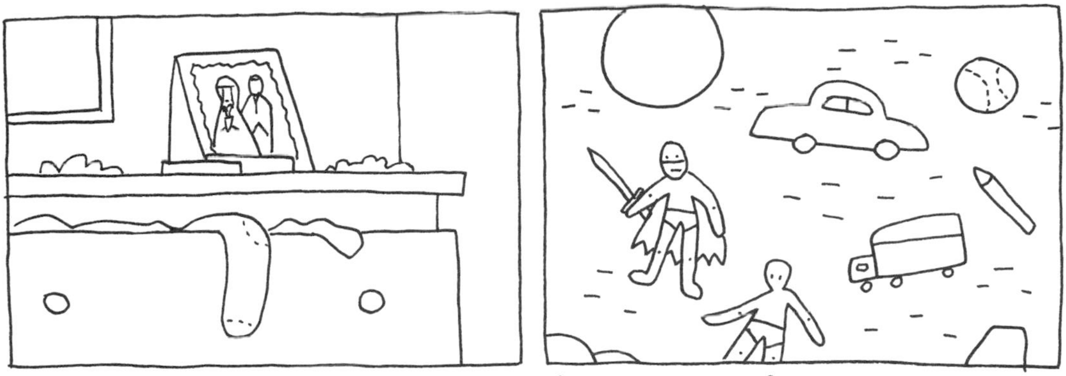

I got married when I was 20.
She had a son. We later had a daughter.

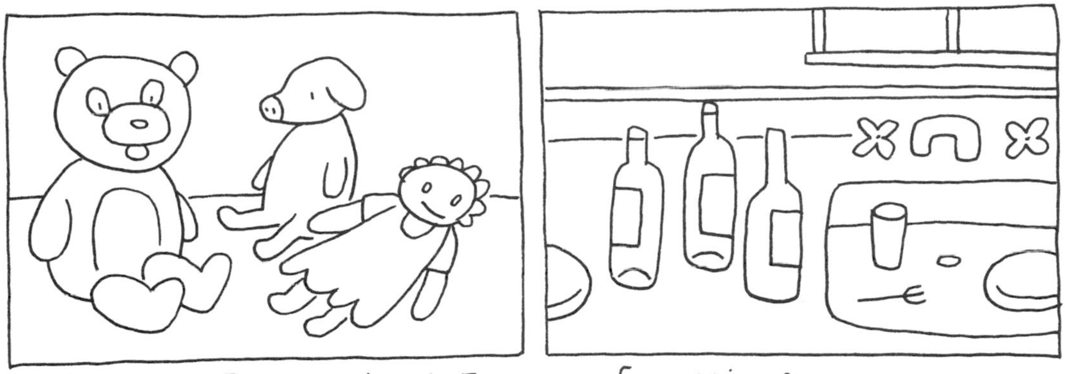

After about 5 years of marriage,
I started feeling she was taking advantage of me.

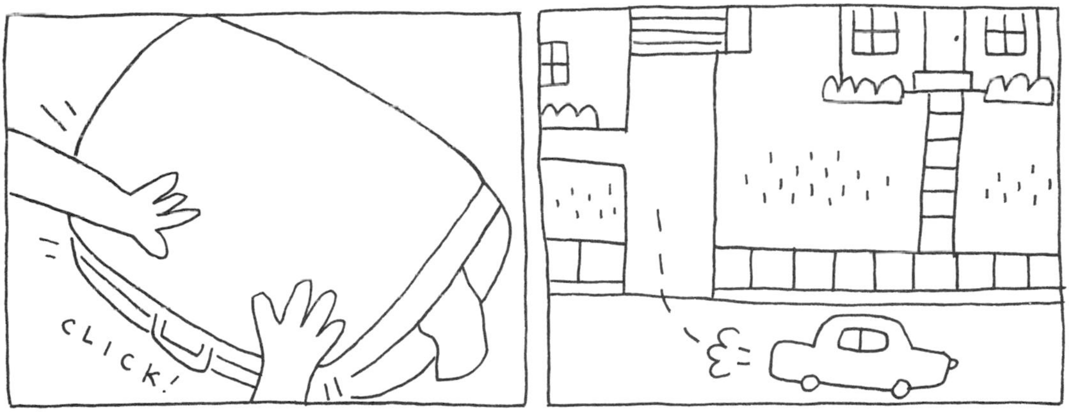
CLICK!

Eventually, we had to call it quits...

Ryan

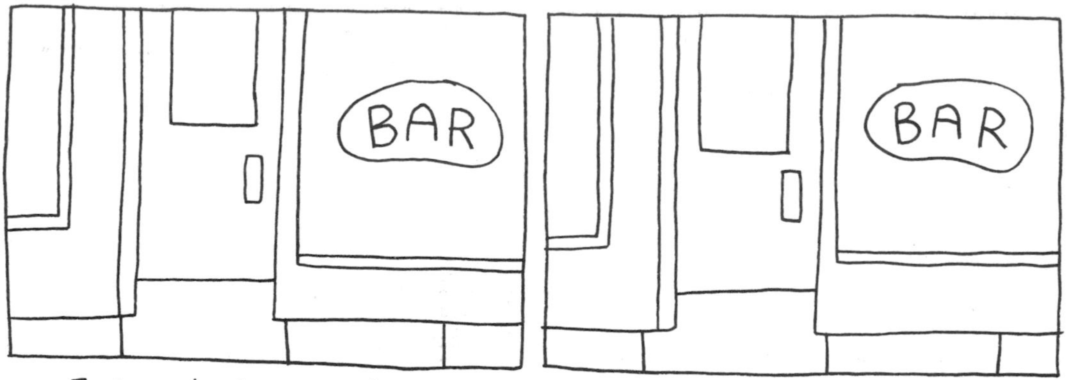
BAR
BAR

I drank too much one night, and somebody attacked me.
I was too drunk to defend myself.

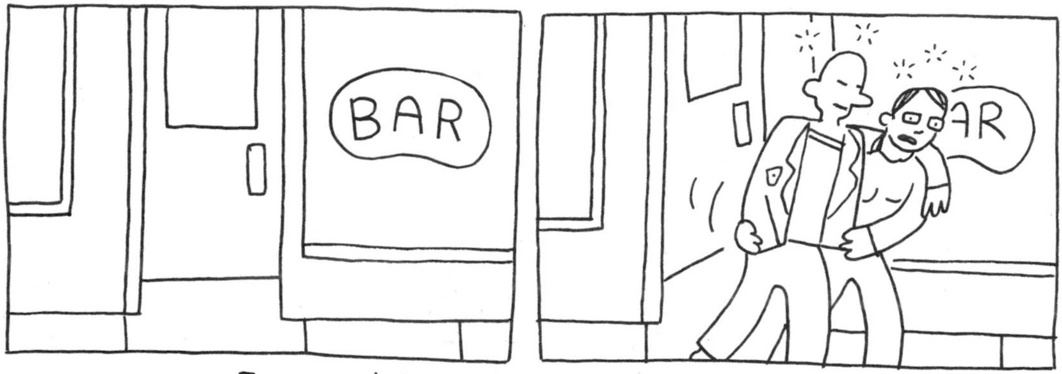
BAR

I was doing a lot of reckless things
that could so easily have gotten me killed...

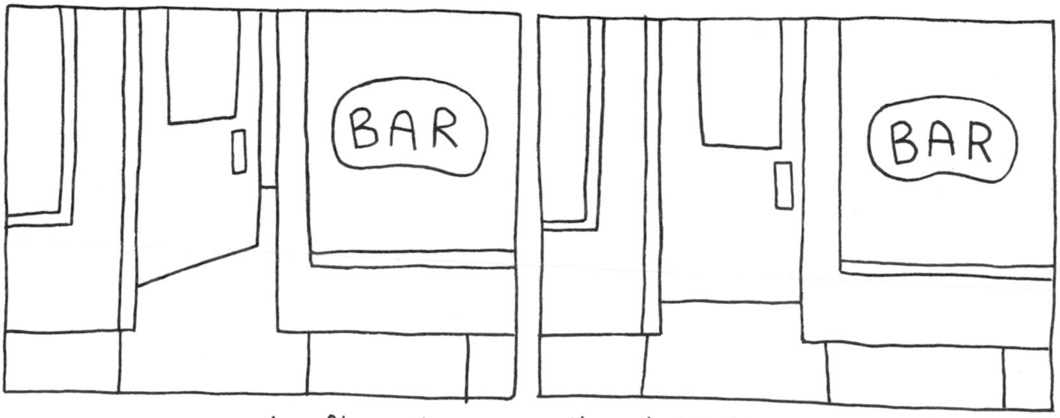
BAR
BAR

...and after the rape, it got 10 times worse.

Tina

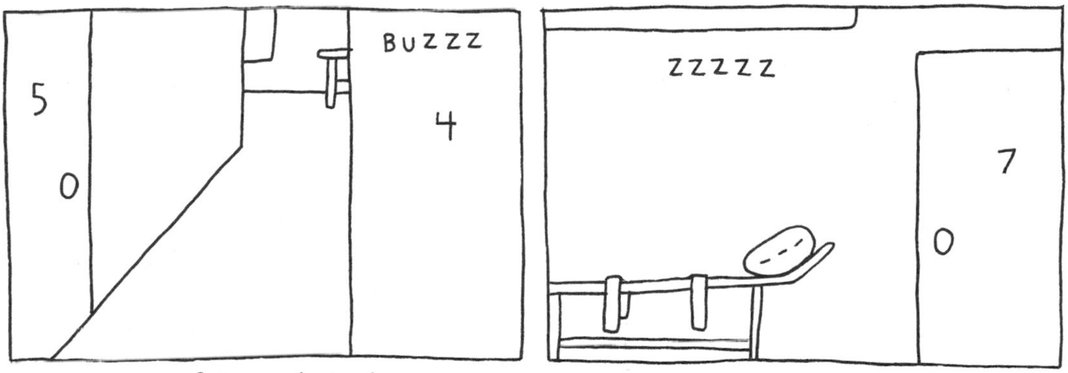
BUZZZ
ZZZZZ

My drinking was getting out of control.
I was in and out of rehab, on and off medication...

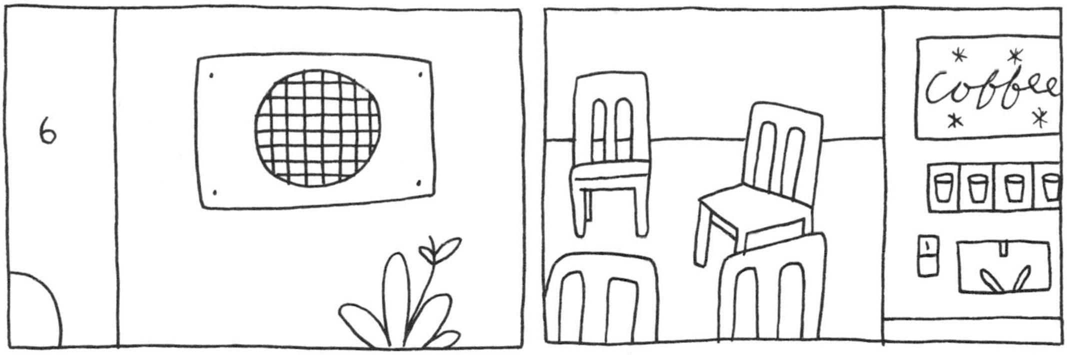
Coffee

While I was in rehab, I met someone, and we started dating.
He later became my fiancé.

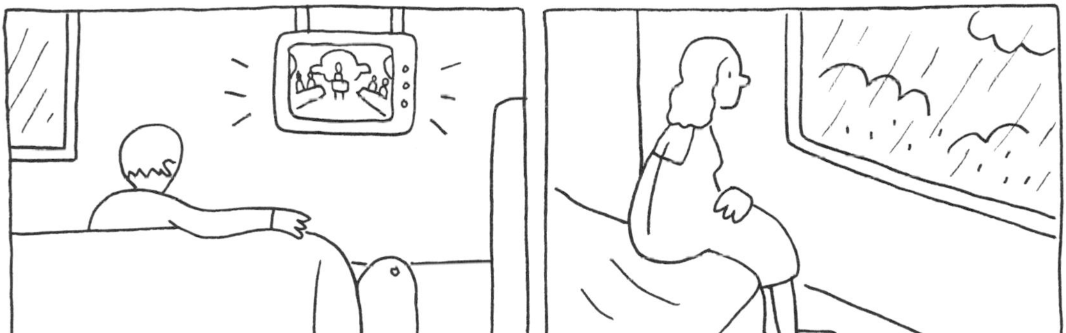

I relate myself a lot to love...
So when I'm not loved, I feel like a big failure.

Chantel

Things were spiraling out of control for me. I drove drunk with my children in the car.

There was a flash in my mind. I saw something coming.

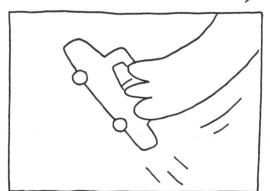

I dropped them off at home. I told them I hoped that the next time I saw them things would be better...

Ryan

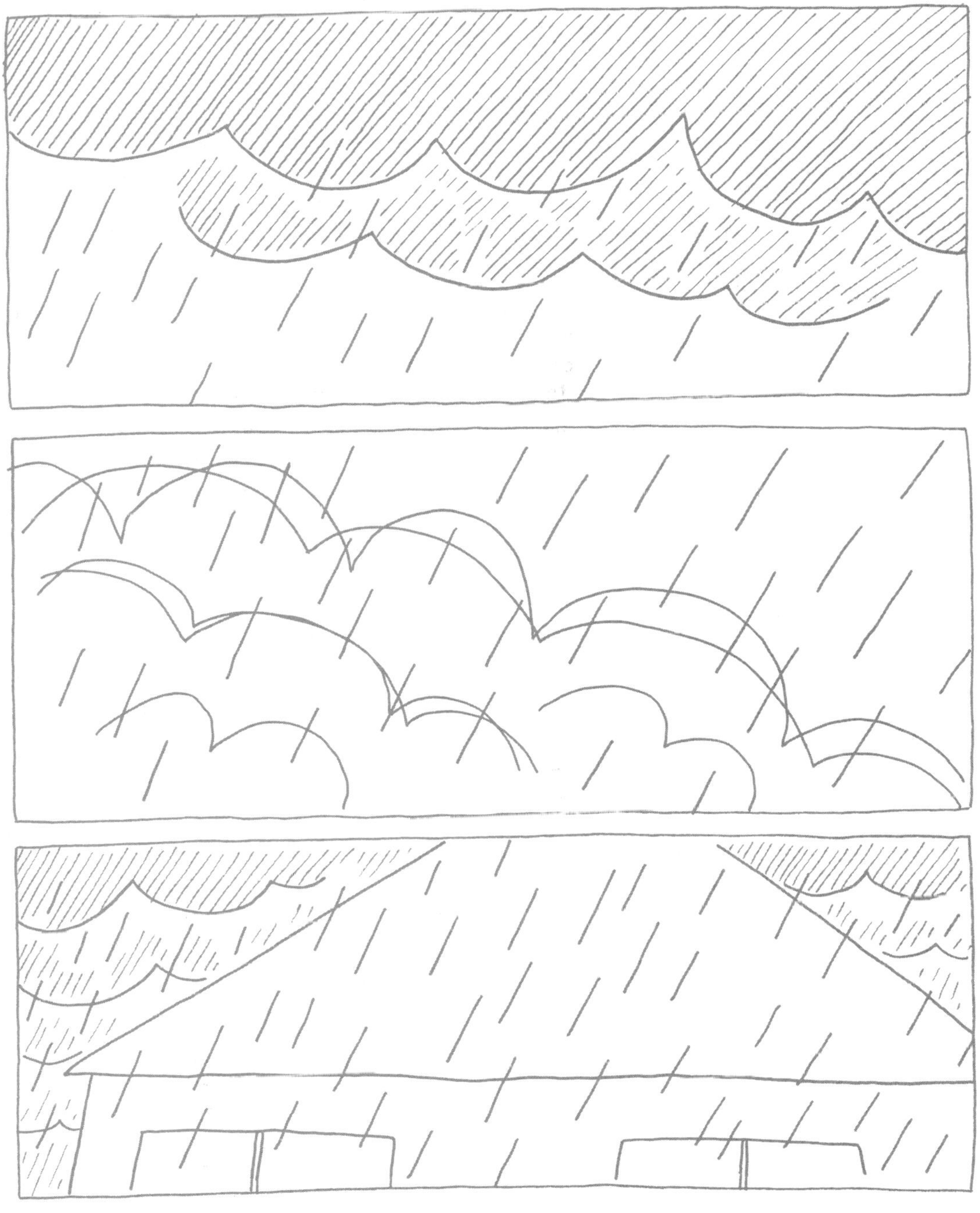

vii.

I was constantly _constantly_ _yelling_ at the voice in my head.

It's a real _voice_... but it's your _own_ reality.

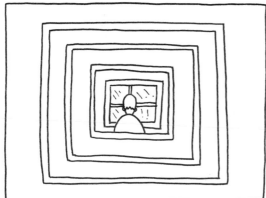

We're all living in our own reality.

Ryan

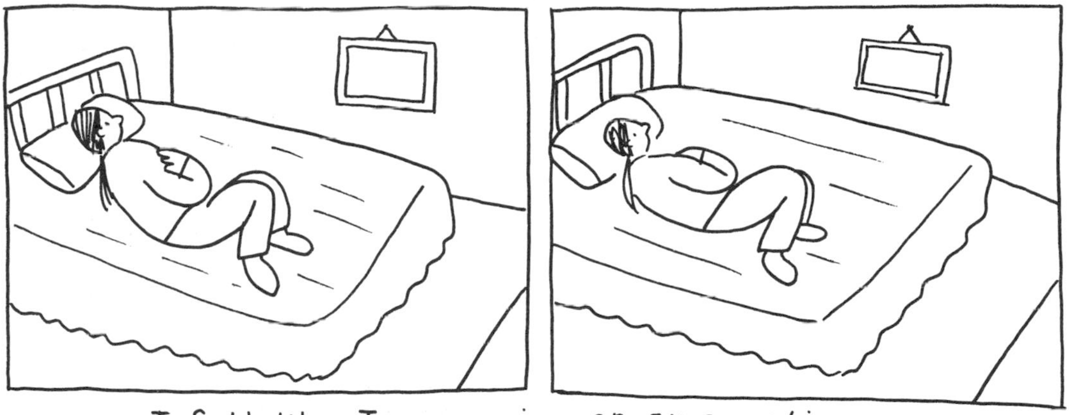

I felt like I was going crazy sometimes.

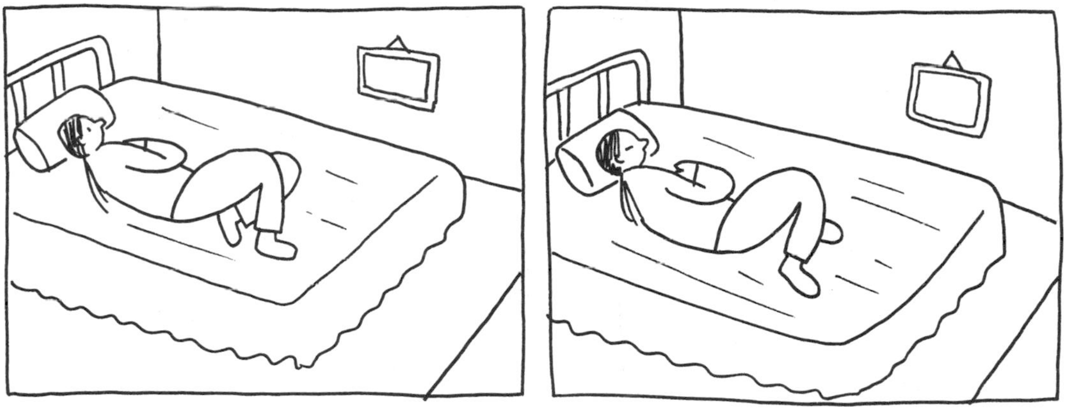

Once, when I was 18 years old, I couldn't get out of bed for 3 days.

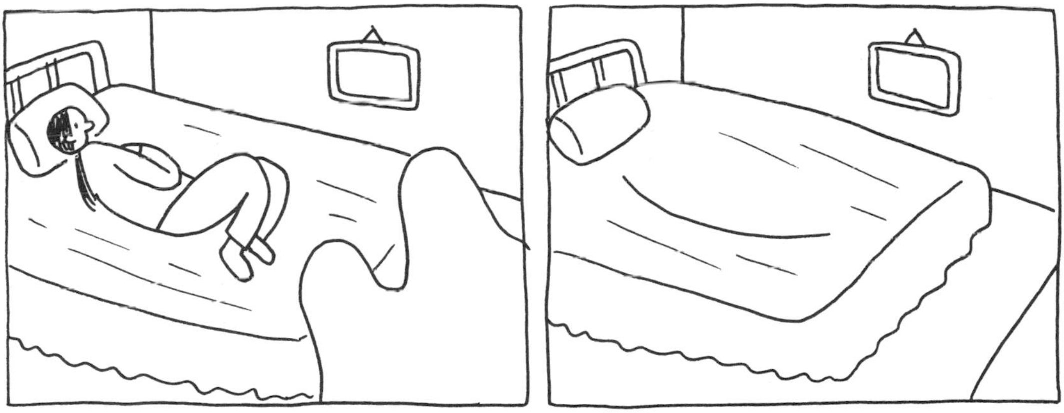

I just lay in bed and cried, until my parents took me to the doctor.

Tina

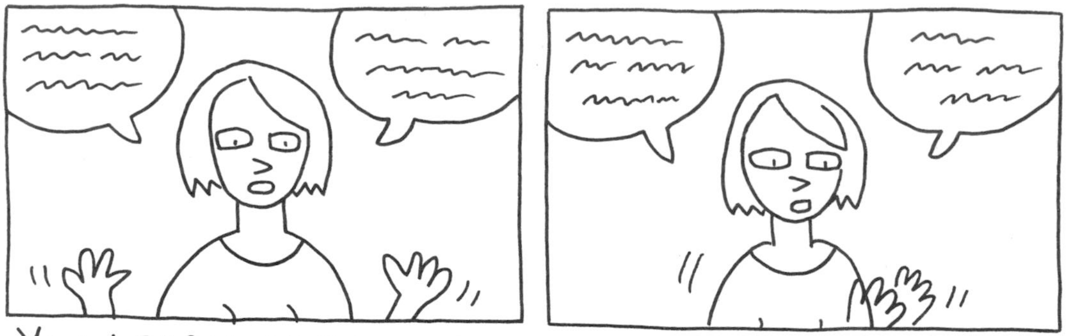

YOU LEARN QUITE QUICKLY THAT YOU CAN SAY WHATEVER YOU WANT TO A THERAPIST, AND THEY'RE JUST GOING TO PAT YOU ON THE HEAD.

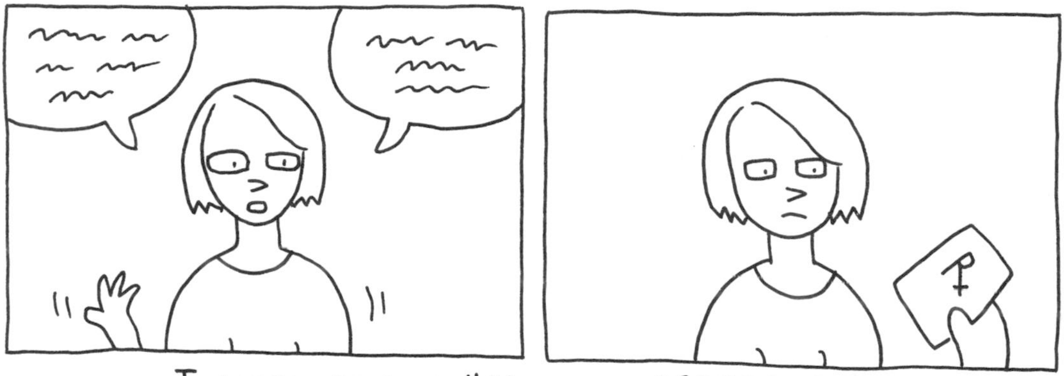

I KEPT SAYING "I'M NOT DEPRESSED! I HAVE <u>ISSUES</u> I NEED TO <u>DEAL</u> WITH!"

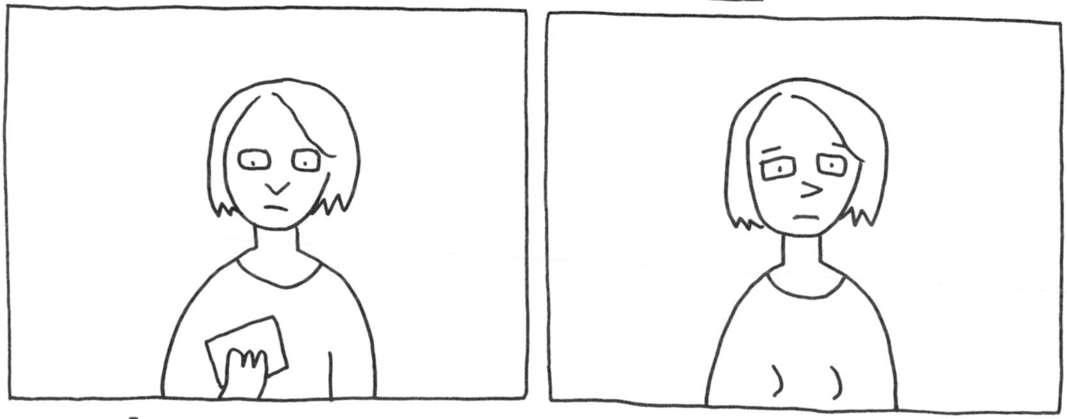

ALL THEY WANTED TO DO WAS DRUG ME UP.

JENN

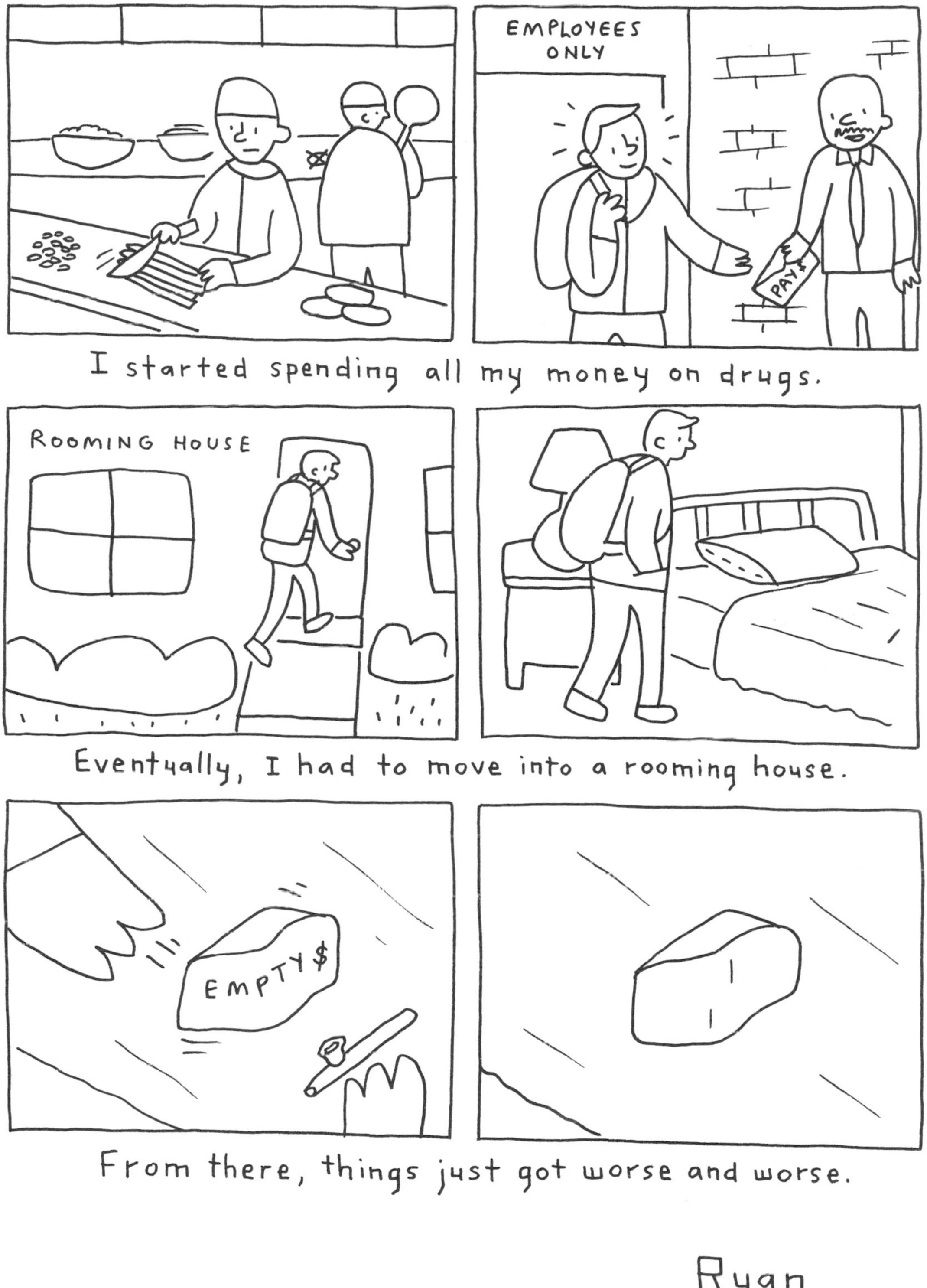
EMPLOYEES ONLY
PAY$
I started spending all my money on drugs.
ROOMING HOUSE
Eventually, I had to move into a rooming house.
EMPTY$
From there, things just got worse and worse.
Ryan

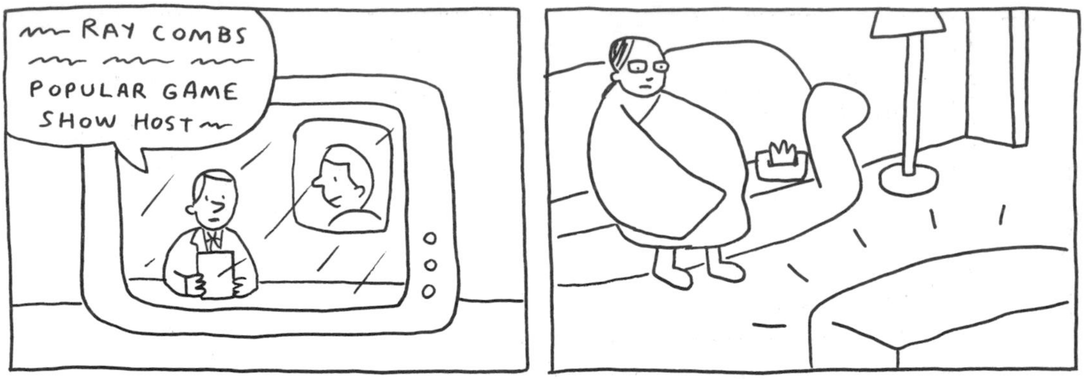
RAY COMBS
POPULAR GAME SHOW HOST

If you had asked me the day before, I would have told you people that kill themselves are taking the easy way out.

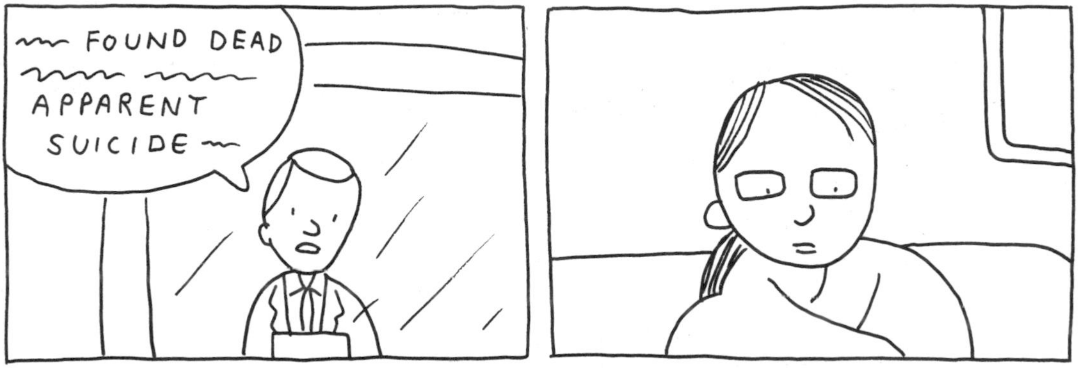
FOUND DEAD
APPARENT SUICIDE

My suicide attempt was a shock, even to myself. It wasn't something I was working up to...

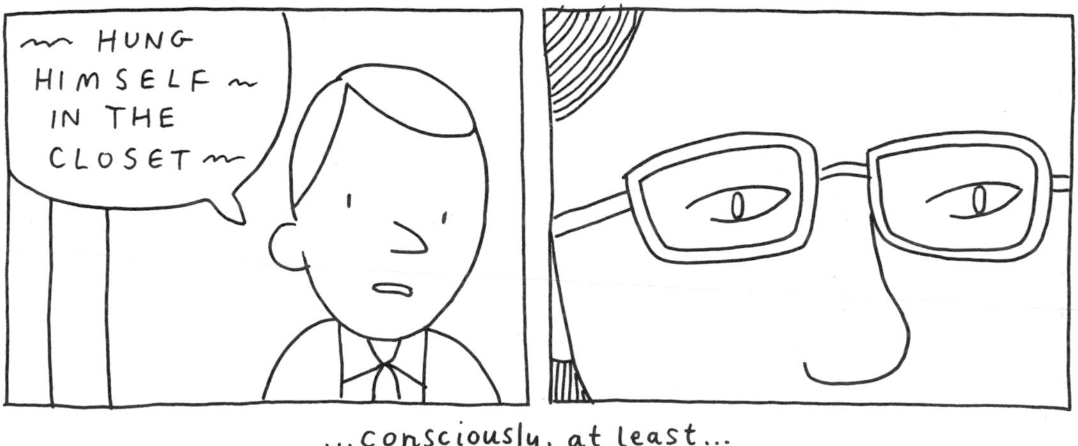
HUNG HIMSELF IN THE CLOSET

...<u>consciously</u>, at least...

Tina

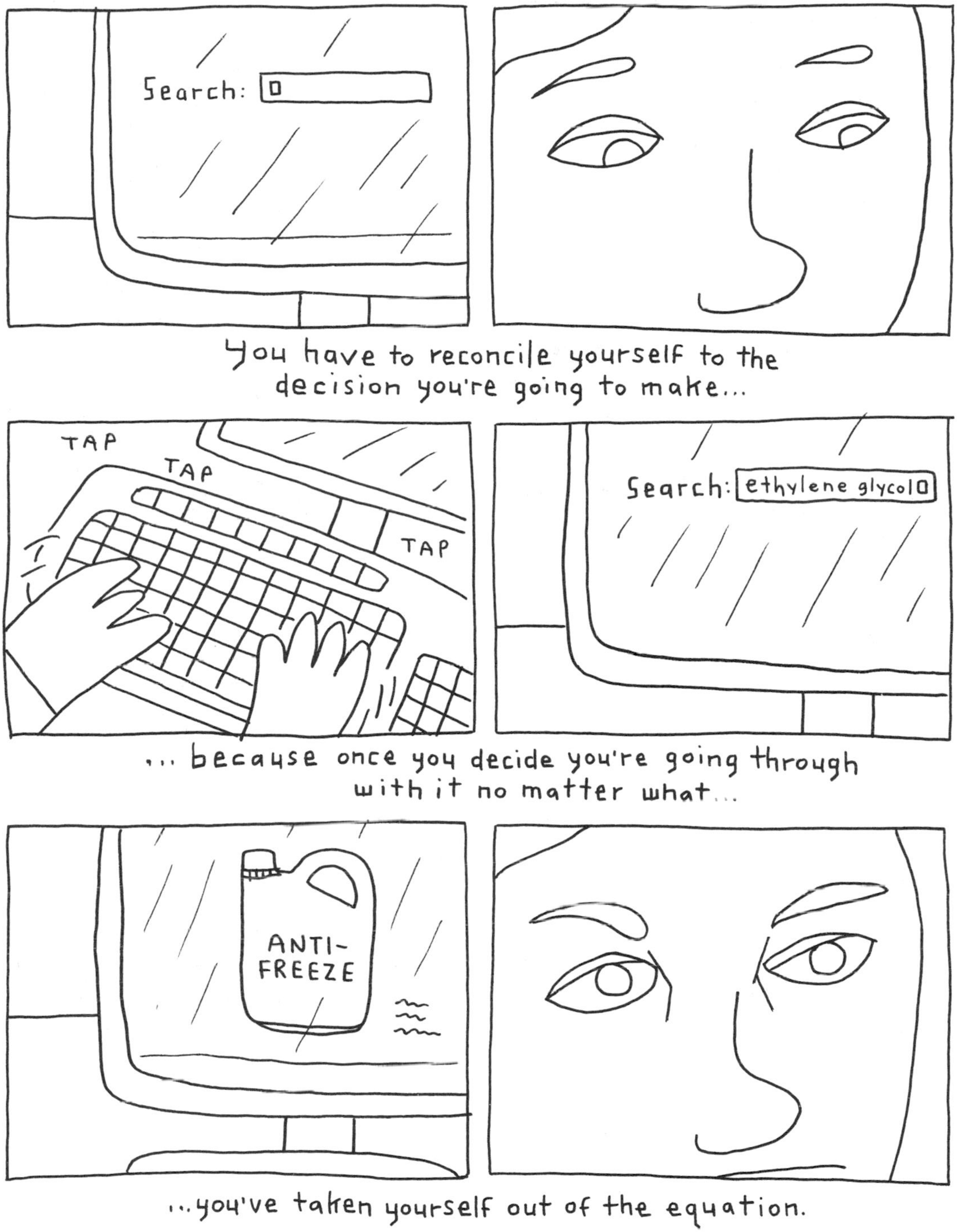
Search:
You have to reconcile yourself to the decision you're going to make...
TAP
TAP
TAP
Search: ethylene glycol
... because once you decide you're going through with it no matter what...
ANTI-FREEZE
...you've taken yourself out of the equation.

Ryan

YOUR SOUL IS COMPLETELY TORN... BUT THE SECOND YOU MAKE THAT CHOICE, YOU FEEL A RUSH OF RELIEF.

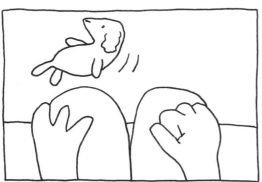

WHEN YOU CAN'T SEE ANY WAY TO CHANGE THE CIRCUMSTANCES YOU'RE IN, DEATH IS A LOGICAL OPTION...

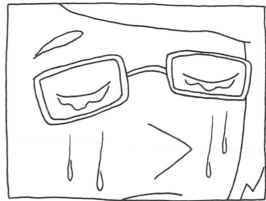

... AND IT BECOMES THE ONLY OPTION.

JENN

 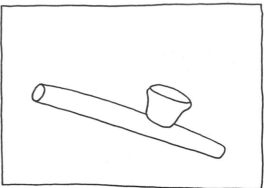

It was after a crack cocaine binge. I had no money left.
I literally locked myself in my room for 3 days.

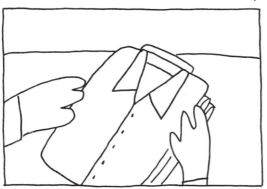 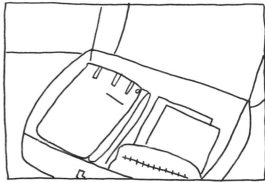

I left several notes. To my mother, to my brother,
and to each of my children.

I just hoped they would forgive me...

Ryan

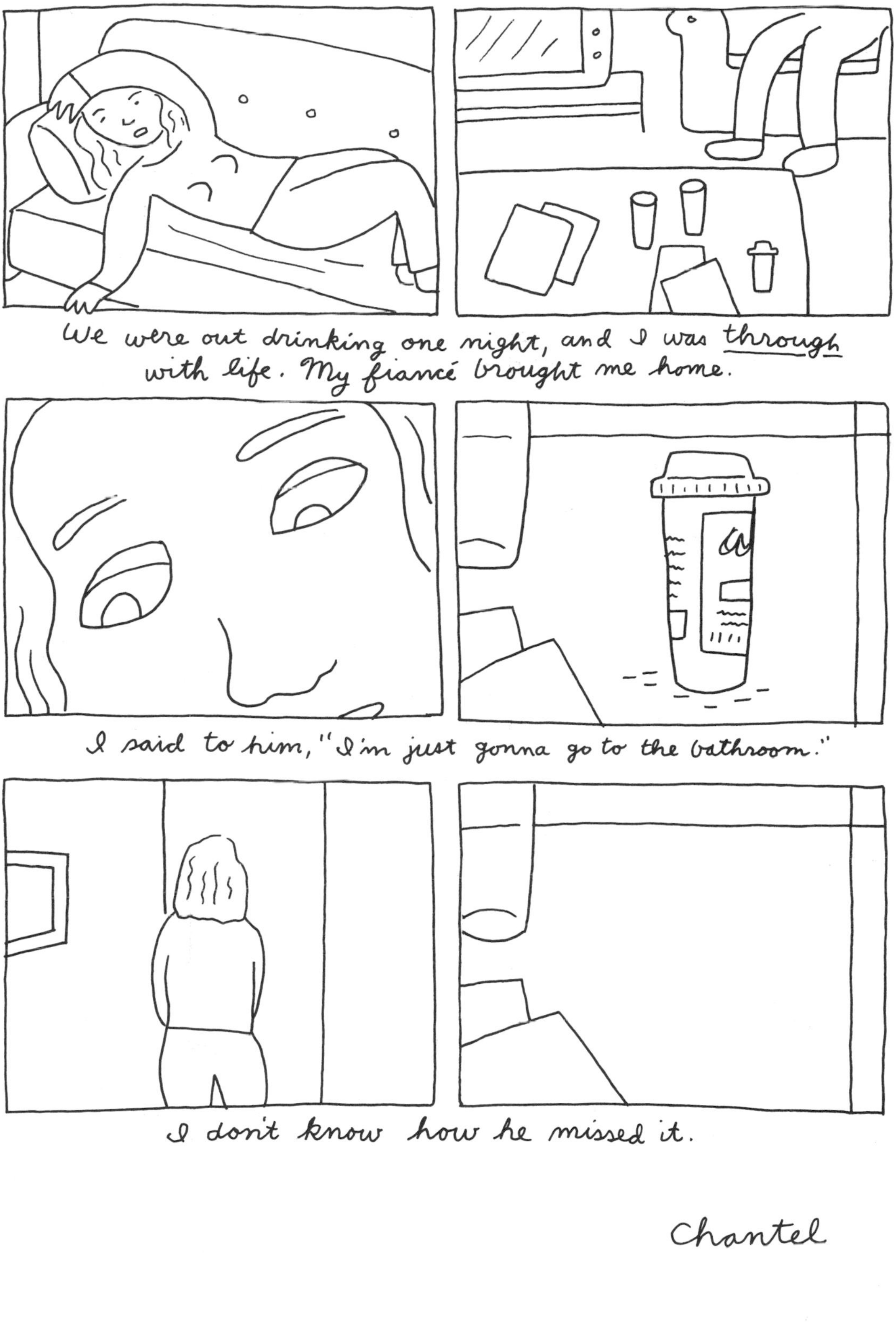
We were out drinking one night, and I was through with life. My fiancé brought me home.
I said to him, "I'm just gonna go to the bathroom."
I don't know how he missed it.
Chantel

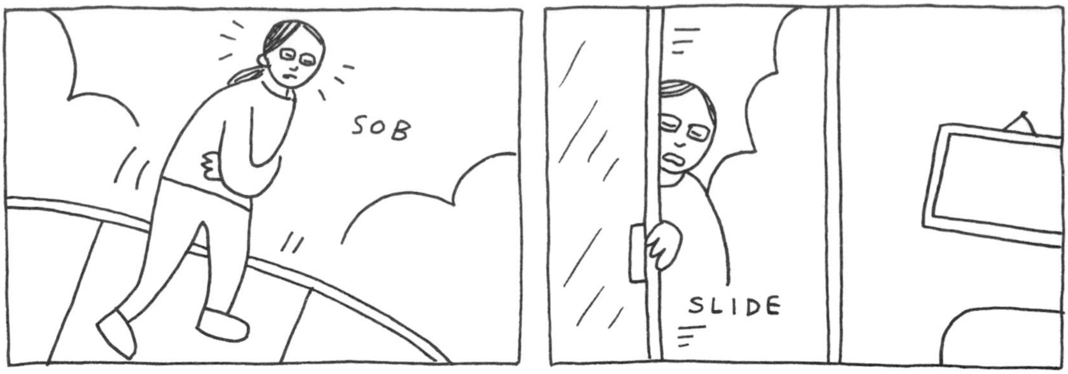
SOB
SLIDE

I was at the bar, and I just started crying. All I could think was "I'm such a loser! I've got to end it..."

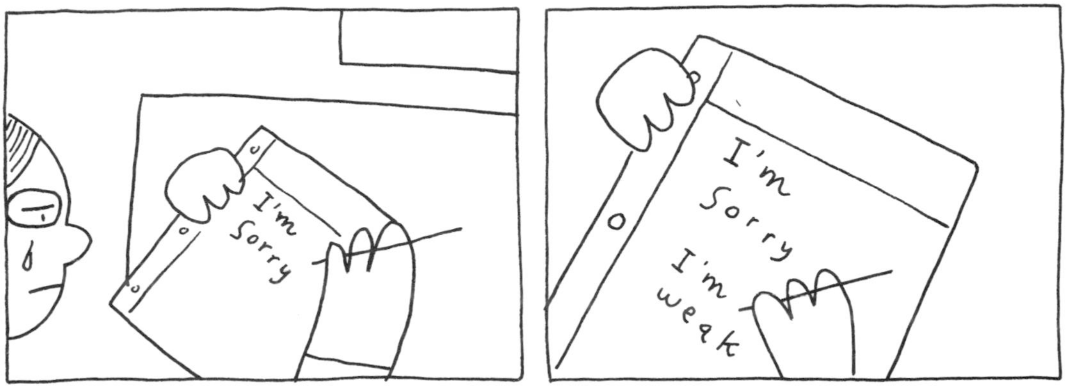
I'm Sorry
I'm Sorry
I'm weak

I ran home alone... I scribbled a note really quickly.

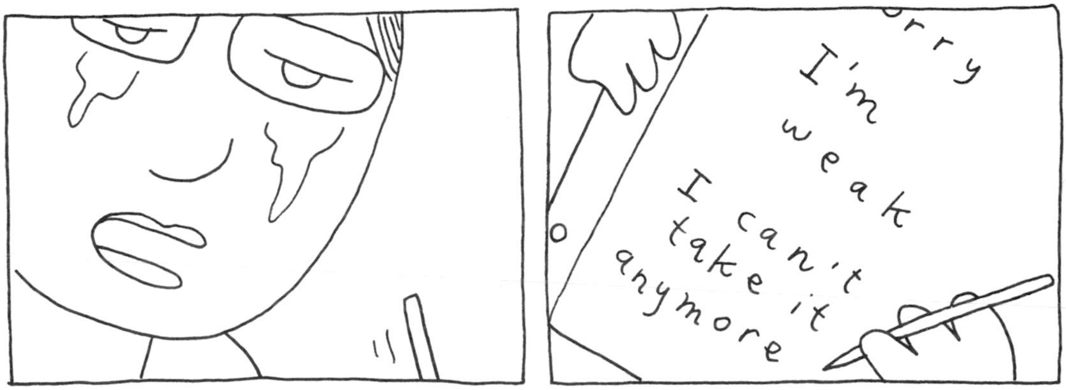
rry
I'm weak
I can't take it anymore

In my whole life, I never seriously thought about suicide... Never.

Tina

My last thought was "Finally!"

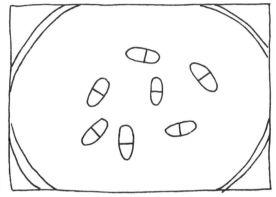

No more pain, no more suffering... just PEACE.

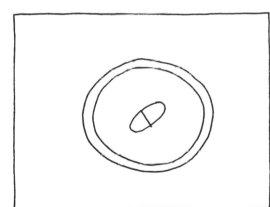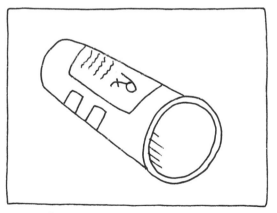

Still... even when you reach that point...

JENN

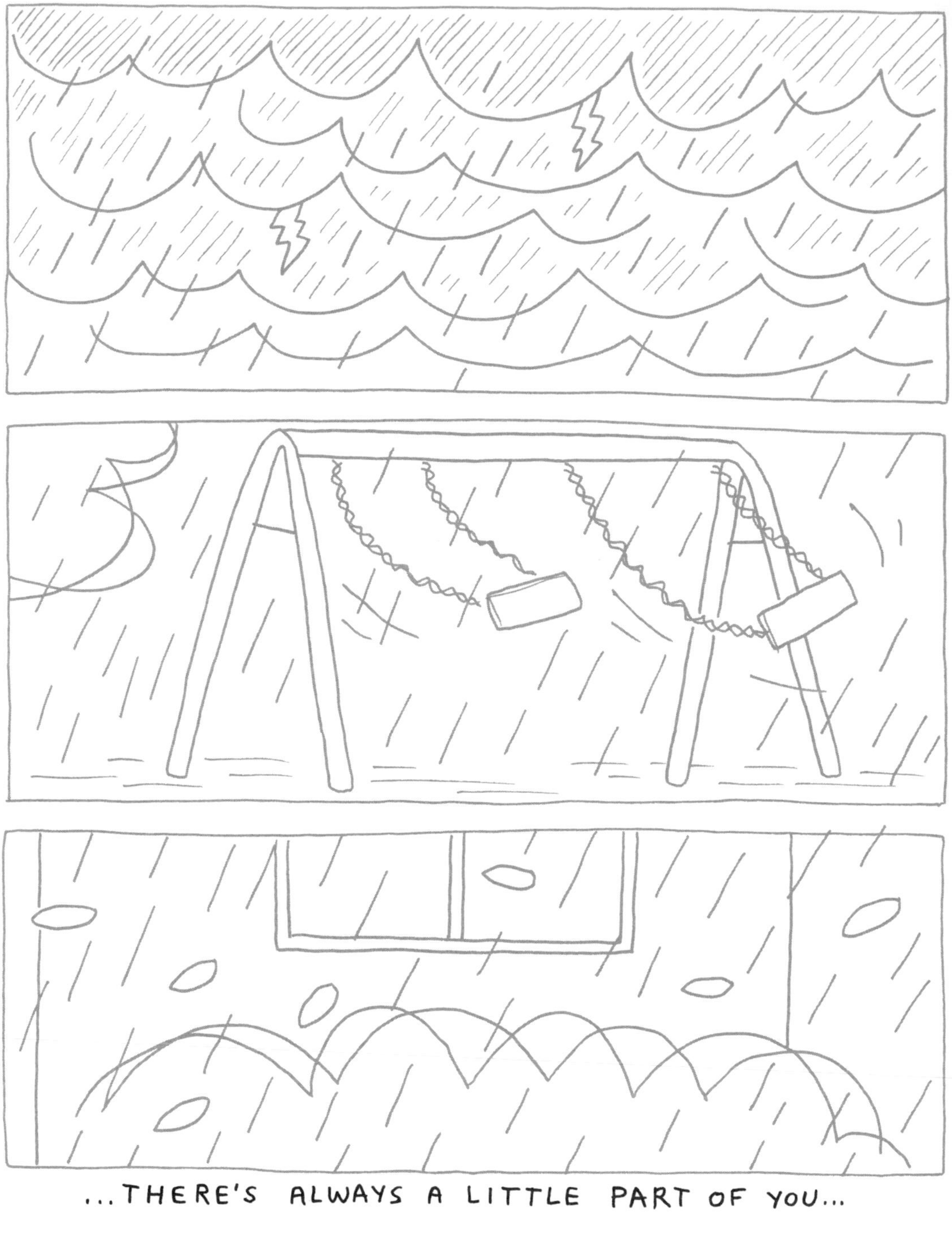

...THERE'S ALWAYS A LITTLE PART OF YOU...

JENN

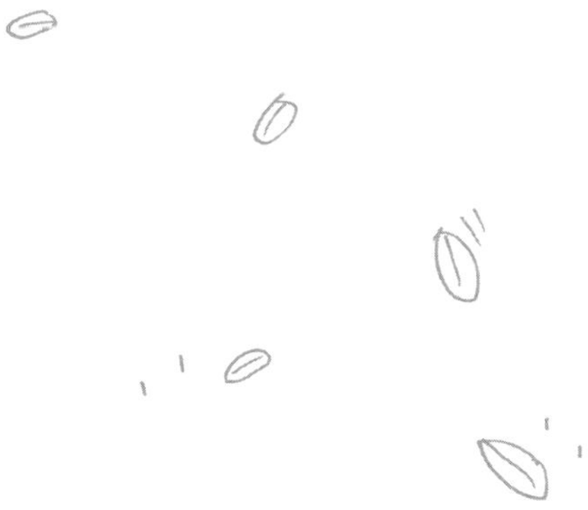

... THAT WISHES IT COULD BE DIFFERENT.

JENN

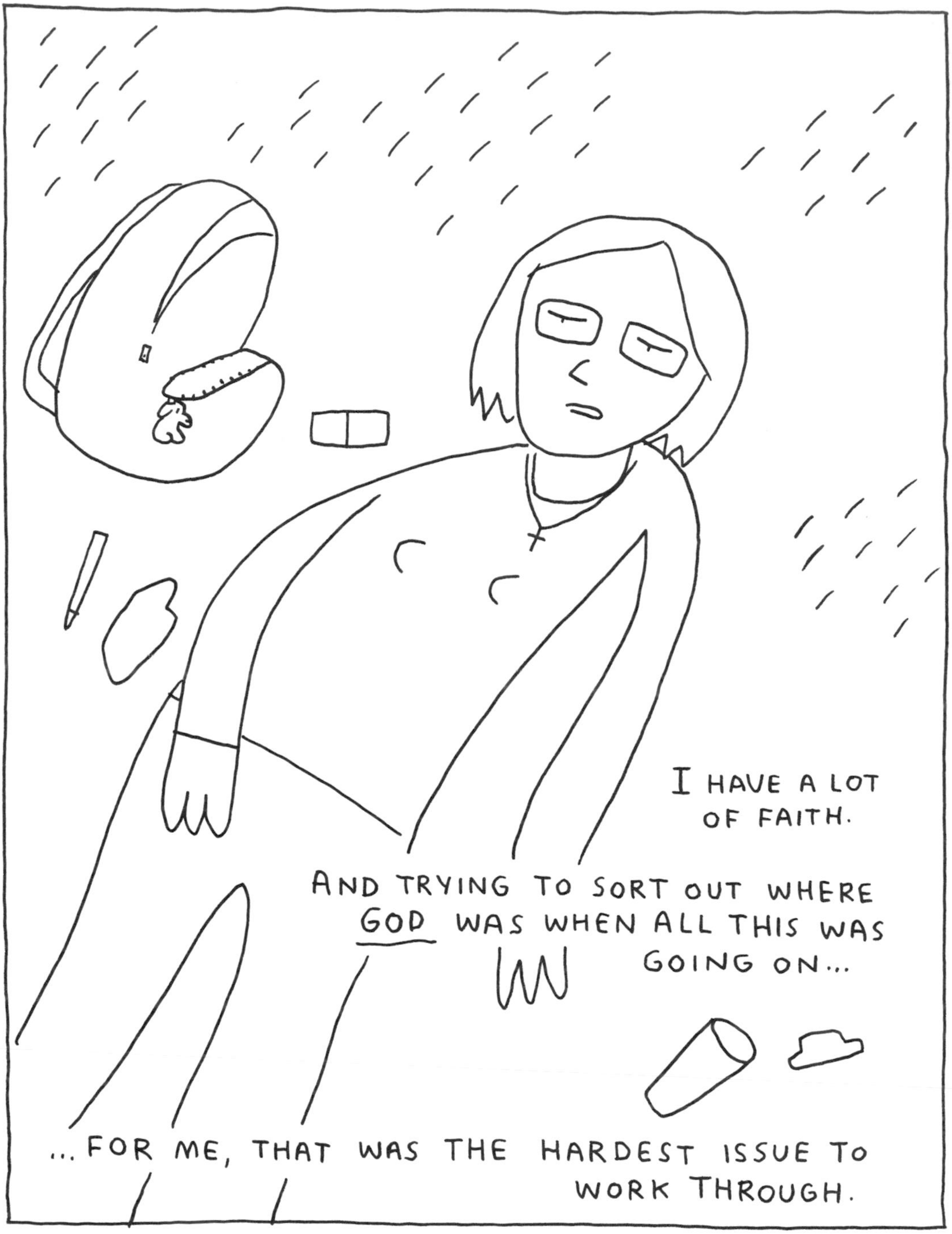
I HAVE A LOT OF FAITH.
AND TRYING TO SORT OUT WHERE GOD WAS WHEN ALL THIS WAS GOING ON...
...FOR ME, THAT WAS THE HARDEST ISSUE TO WORK THROUGH.

JENN

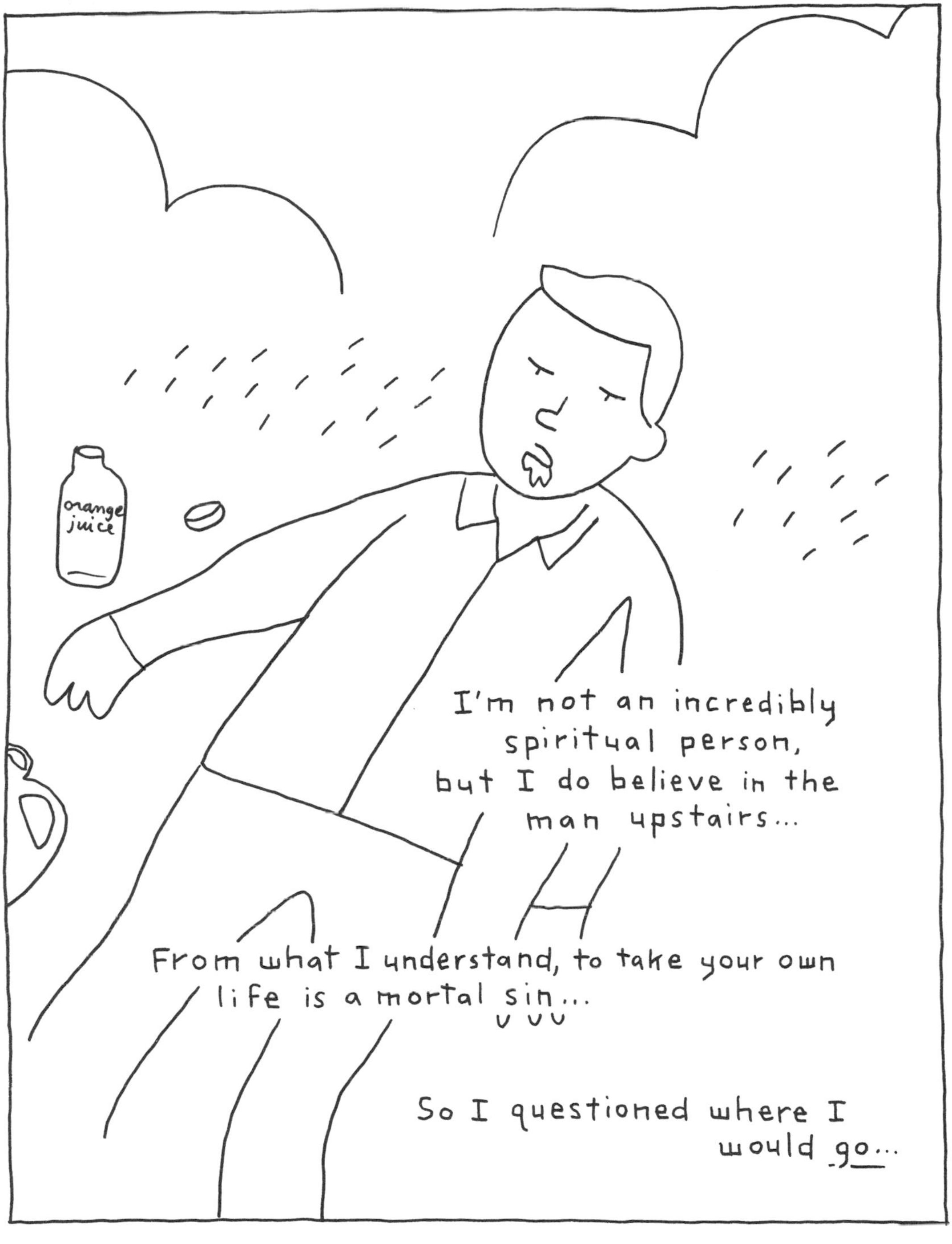
orange juice
I'm not an incredibly spiritual person, but I do believe in the man upstairs...
From what I understand, to take your own life is a mortal sin...
So I questioned where I would go...

Ryan

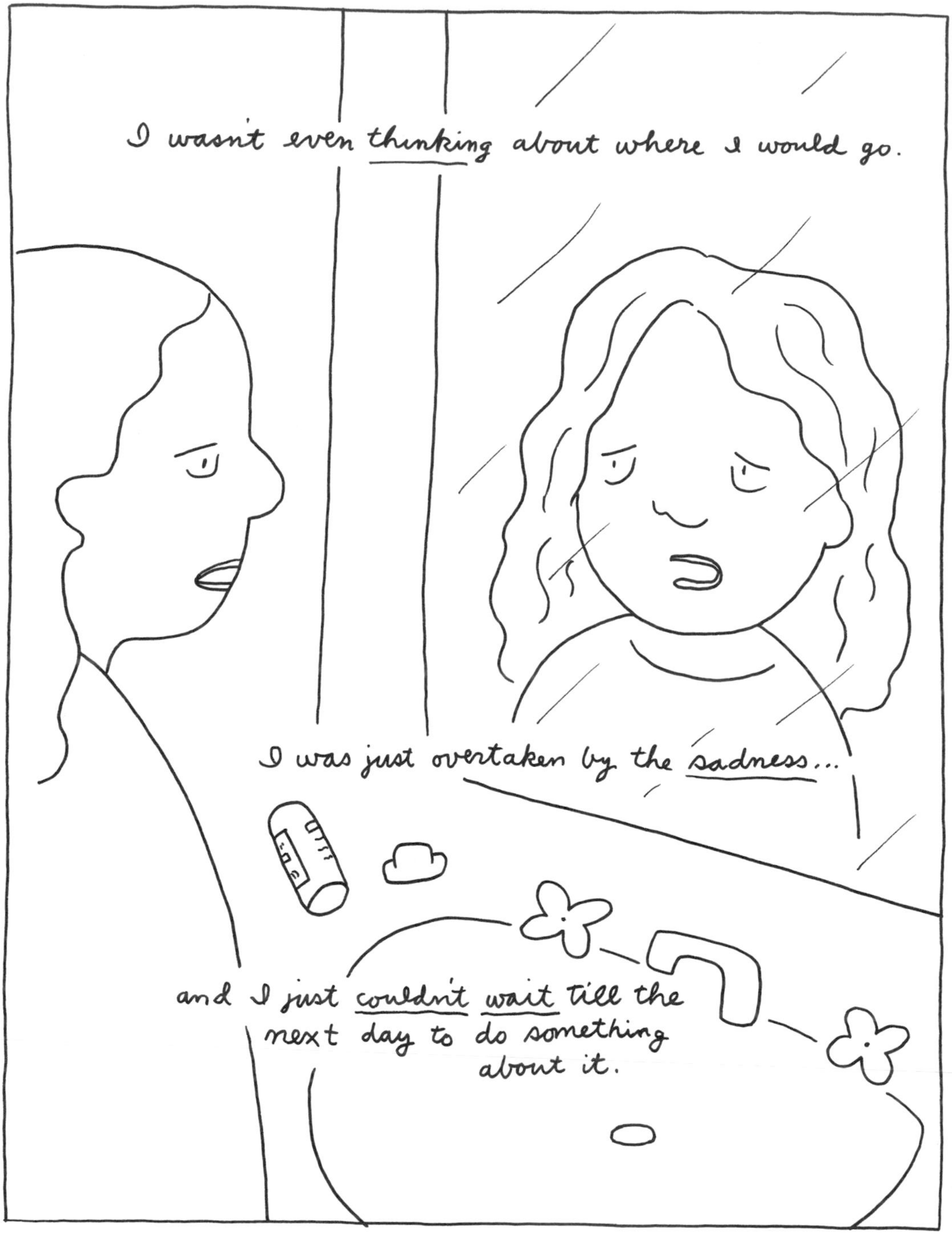
I wasn't even thinking about where I would go.
I was just overtaken by the sadness...
and I just couldn't wait till the next day to do something about it.

Chantel

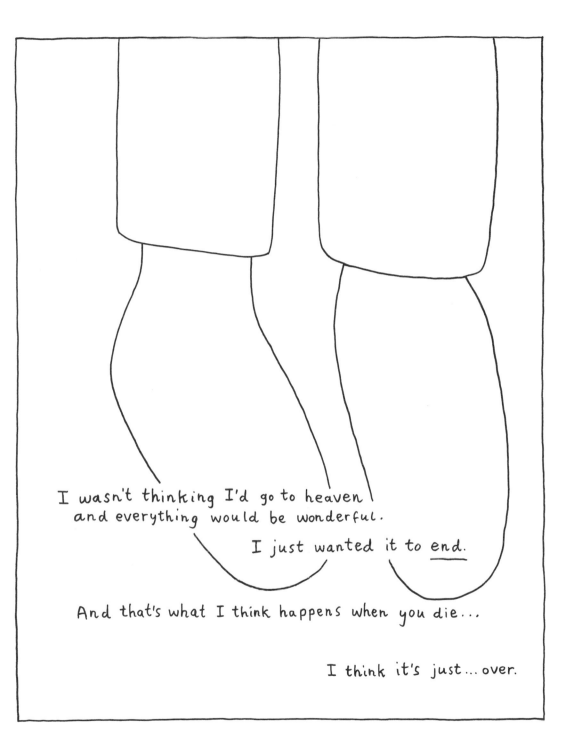

I wasn't thinking I'd go to heaven
and everything would be wonderful.

I just wanted it to end.

And that's what I think happens when you die...

I think it's just... over.

Tina

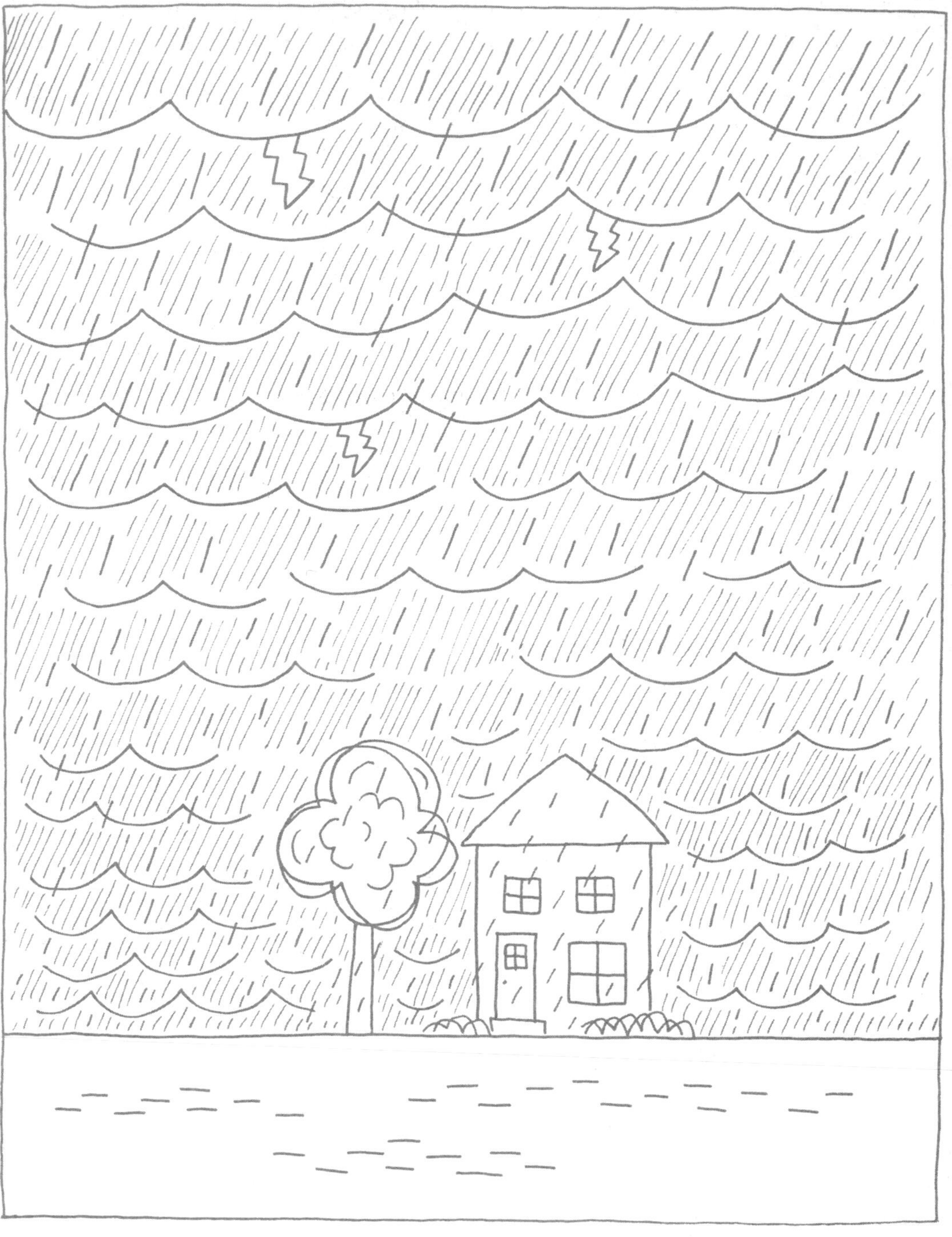

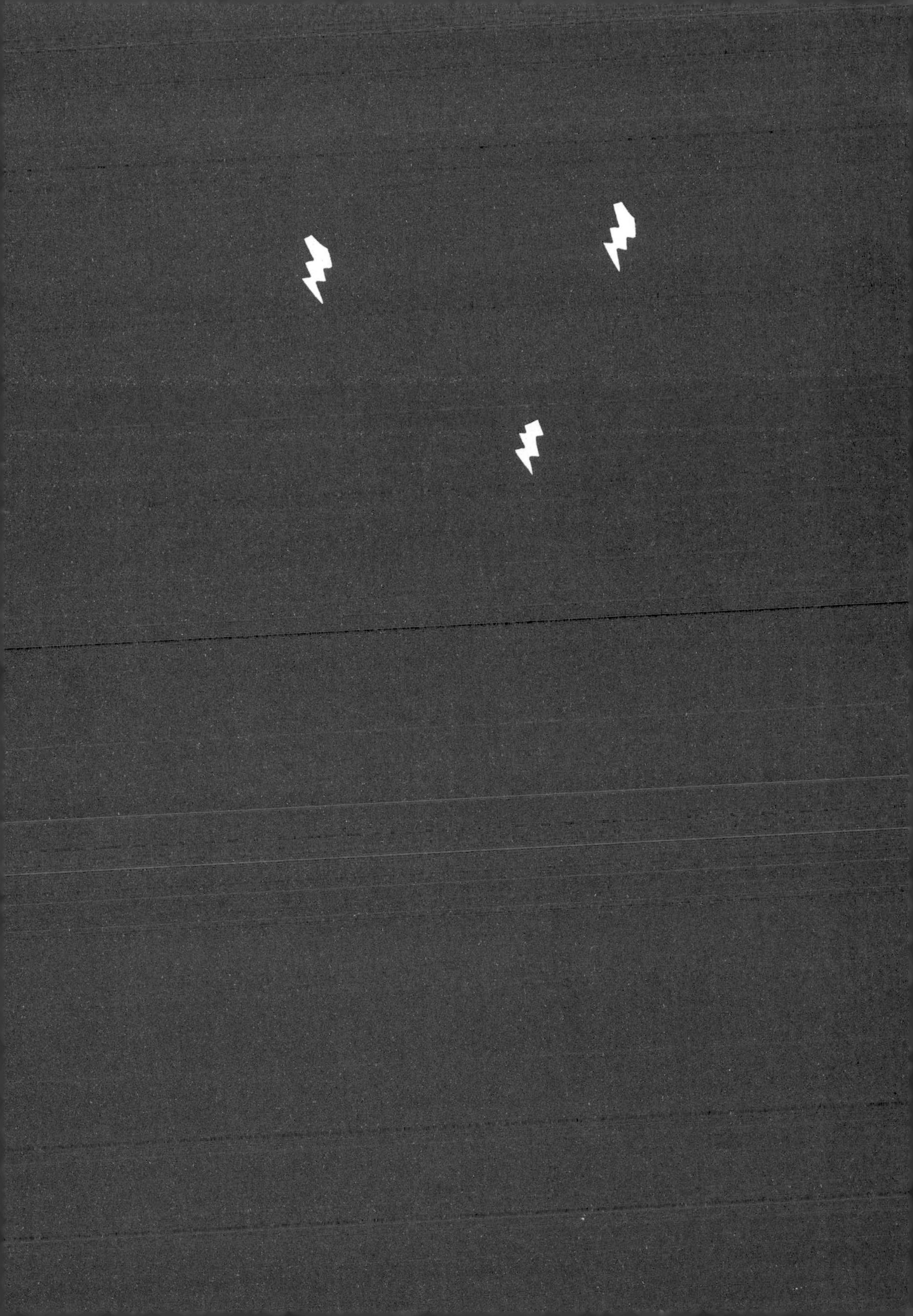

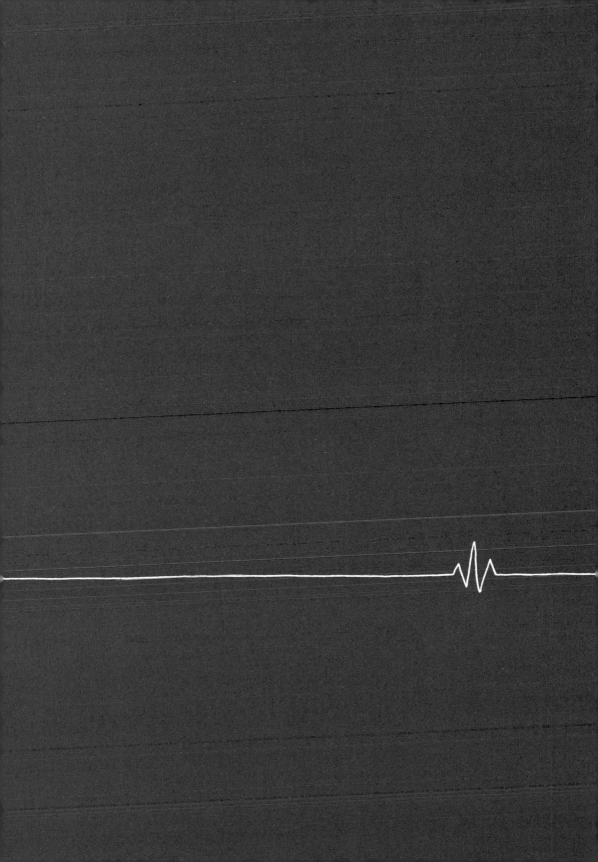

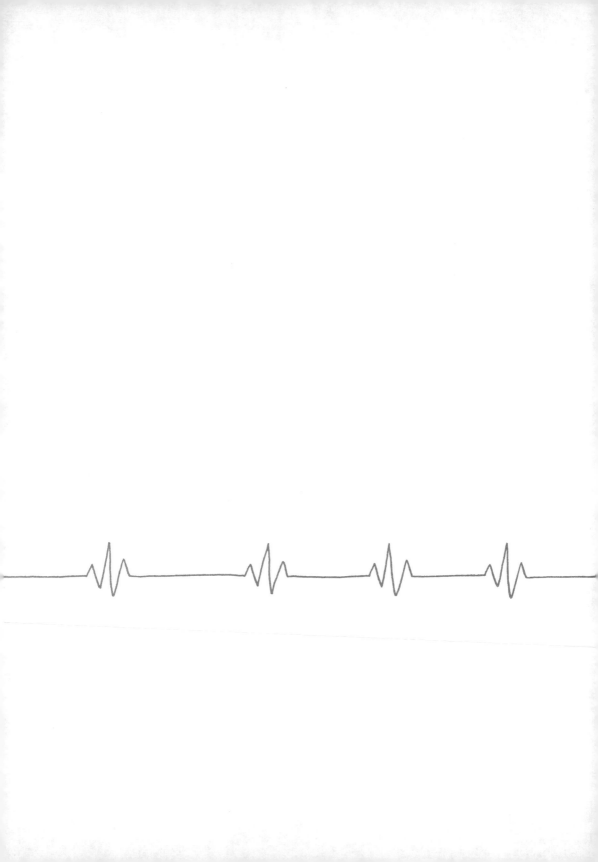

The Next Day...

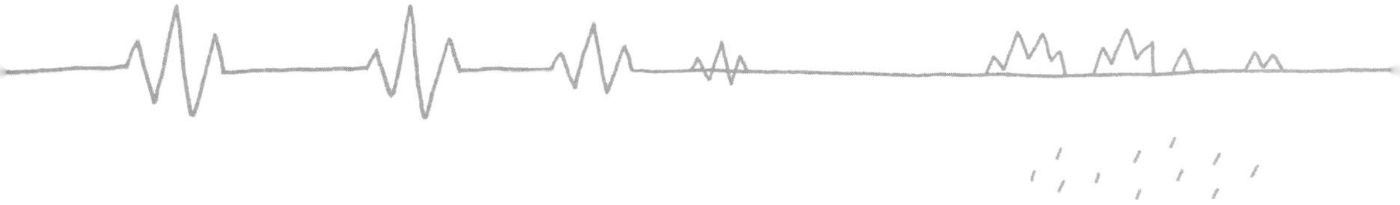

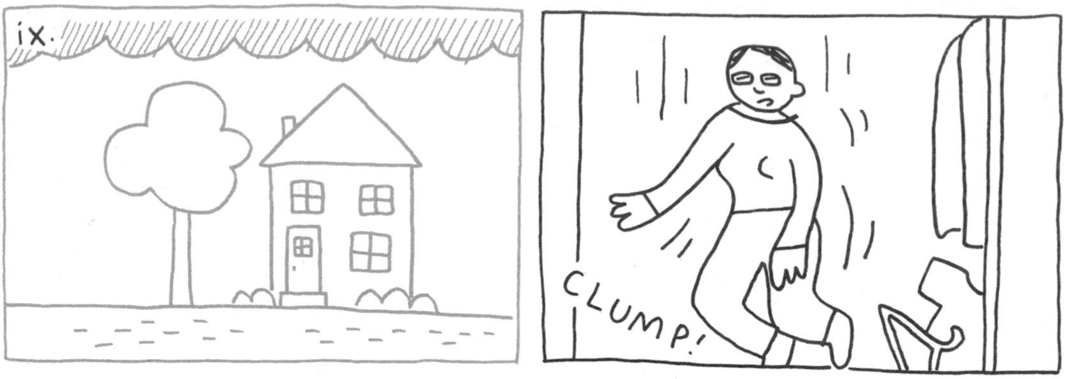
ix.
CLUMP!

As soon as I hit the floor, I just started crying. I thought, "What the hell did I just do?"

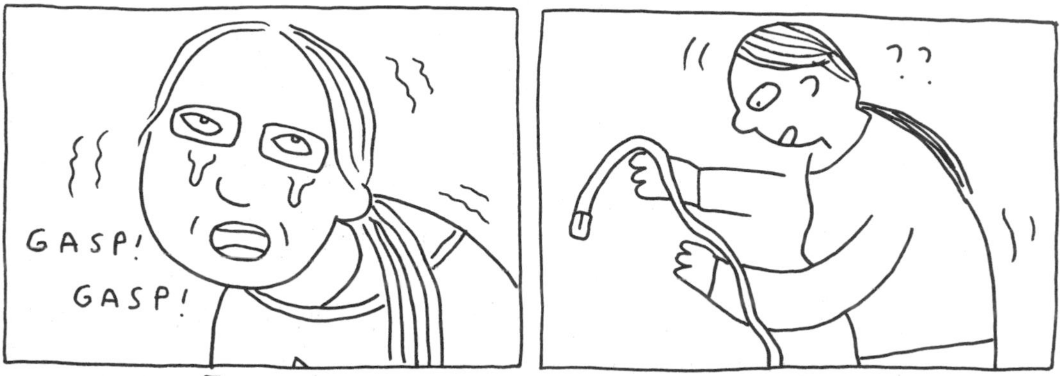
GASP!
GASP!
??

I used to feel a lot of shame. Now I just think, "It wasn't my fault."

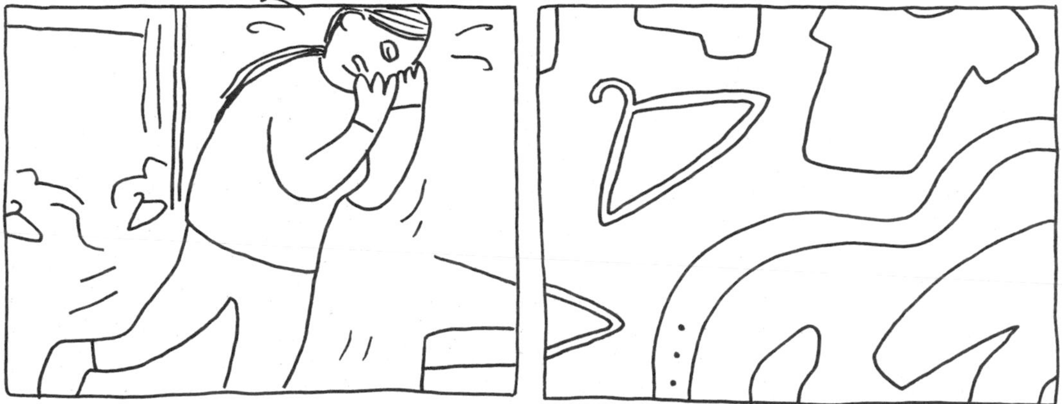

That <u>comforts</u> me.

Tina

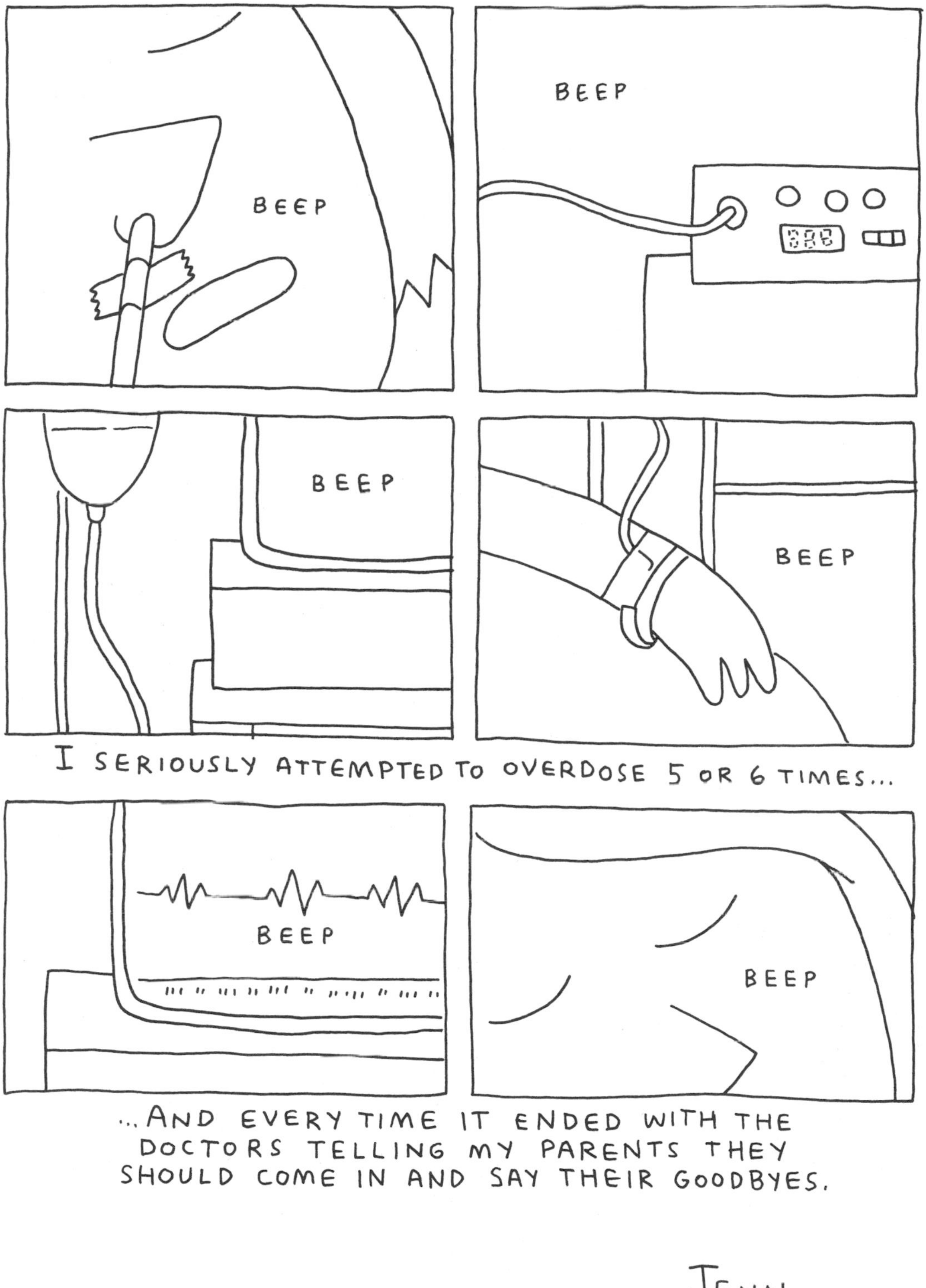
BEEP
BEEP
BEEP
BEEP
I SERIOUSLY ATTEMPTED TO OVERDOSE 5 OR 6 TIMES...
BEEP
BEEP
...AND EVERY TIME IT ENDED WITH THE DOCTORS TELLING MY PARENTS THEY SHOULD COME IN AND SAY THEIR GOODBYES.
JENN

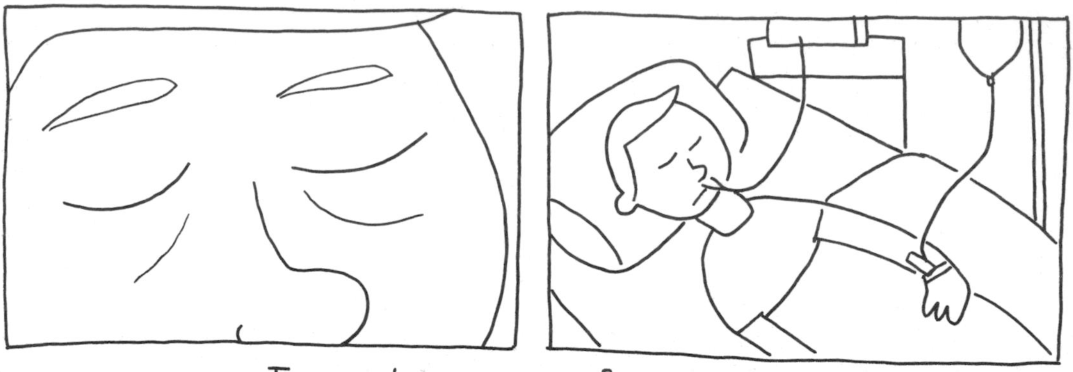

I was in a coma for 17 days.
Every vital organ in my body had completely shut down.

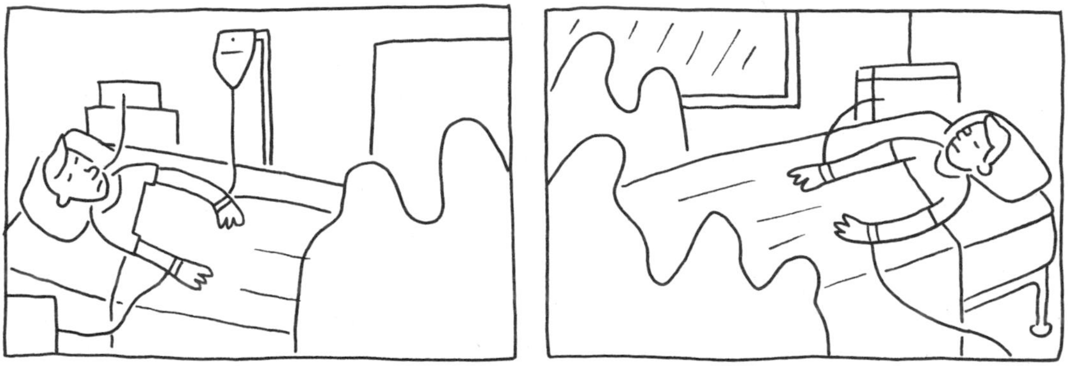

The best part was that the whole family was together for the first time since my parents' divorce.

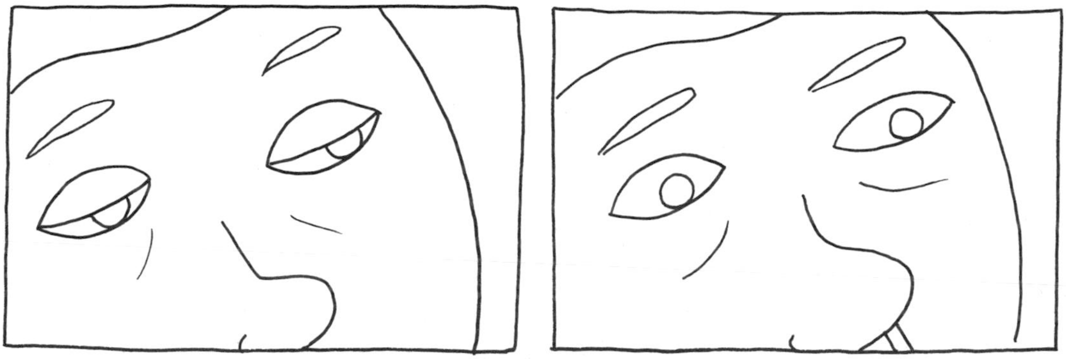

The worst part was having to be restrained after I awoke.
I was so angry I tried to pull out my tubes.

Ryan

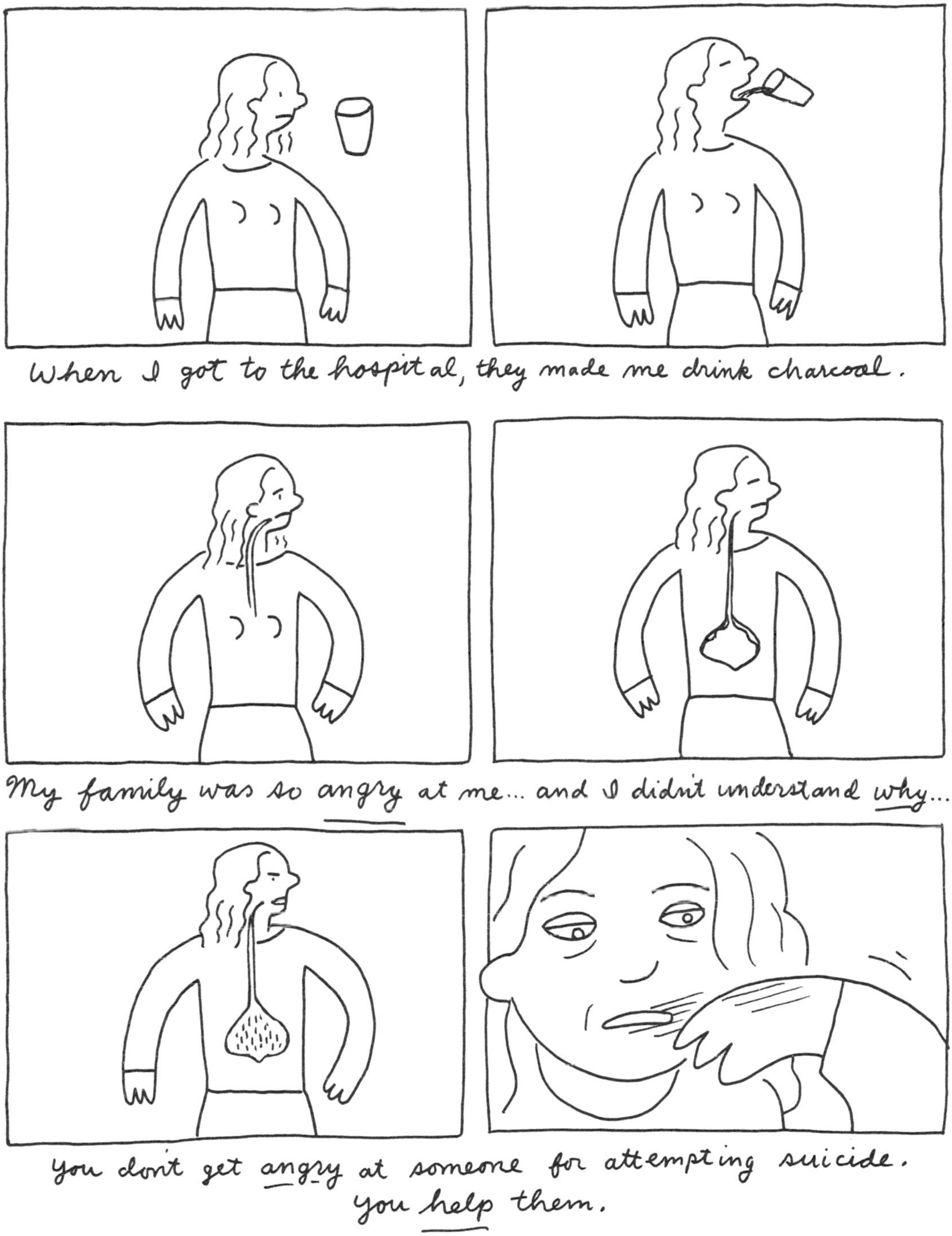
When I got to the hospital, they made me drink charcoal.
My family was so angry at me... and I didnt understand why...
You don't get angry at someone for attempting suicide.
You help them.

Chantel

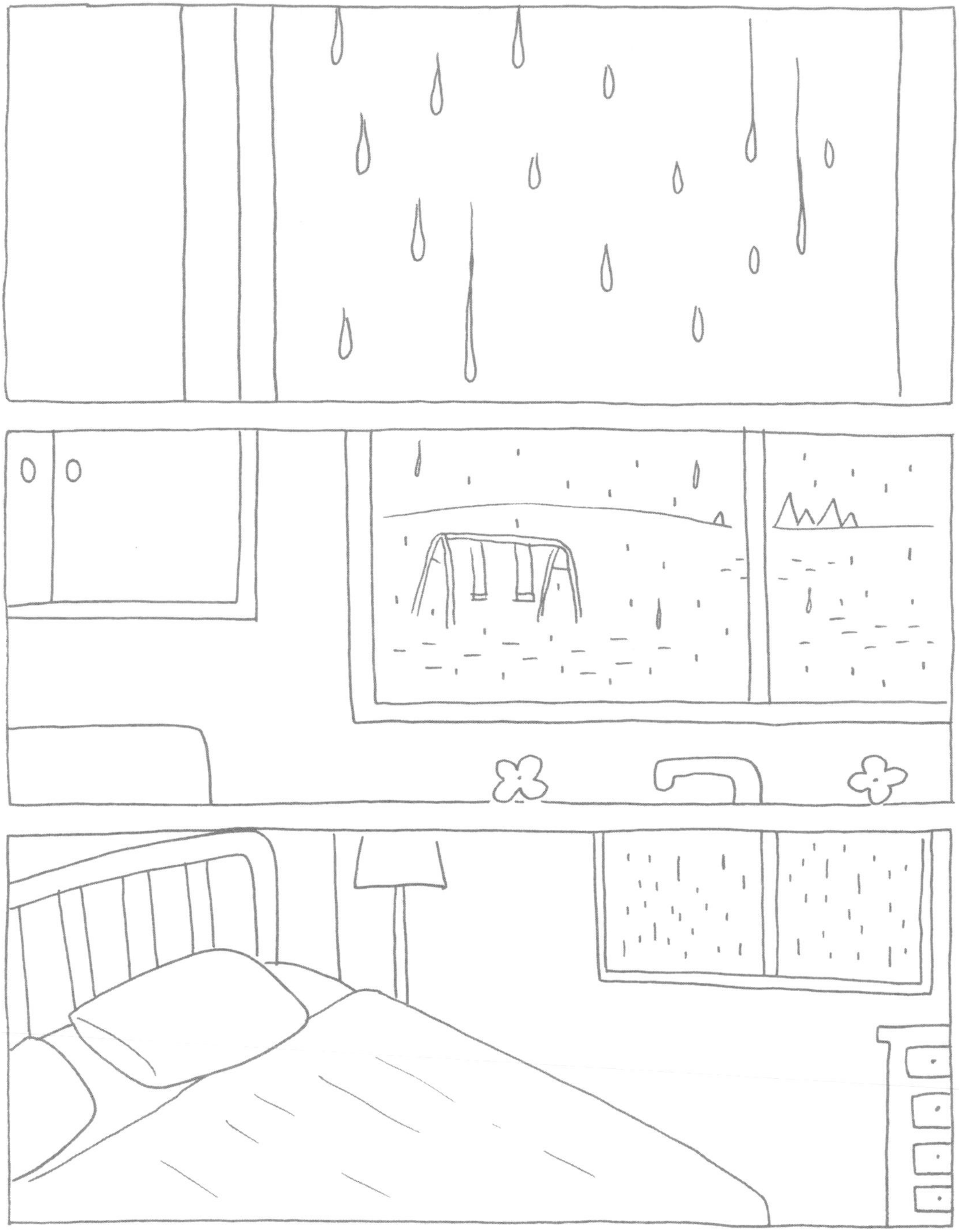

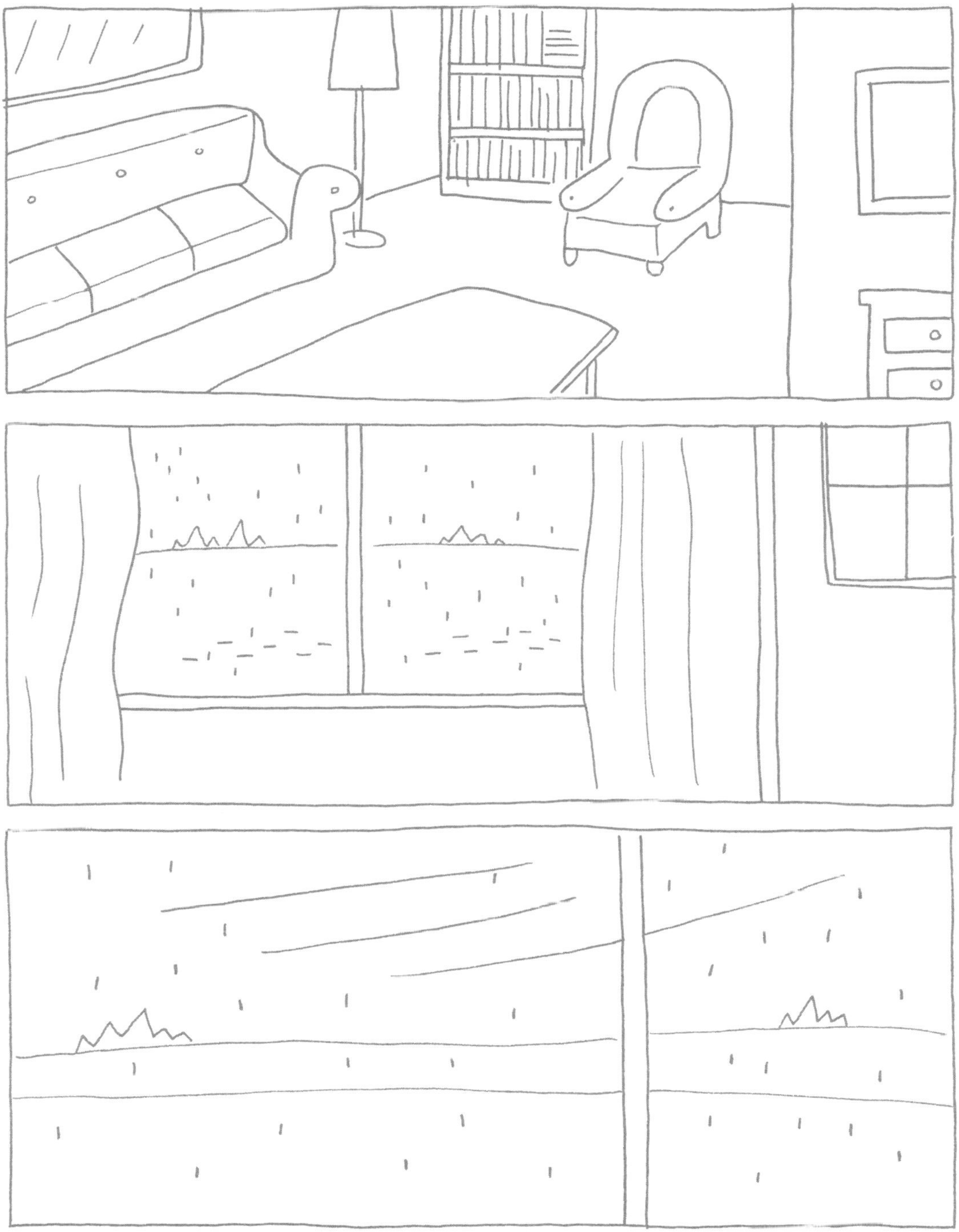

MY KIDS ARE MY BEST MEMORIES SINCE. I WOULD NEVER
HAVE BELIEVED I COULD BE A MOM, OR A WIFE, OR A NURSE.

I'M REALLY GLAD I WASN'T SUCCESSFUL.
I STILL HAVE SO MUCH TO DO...

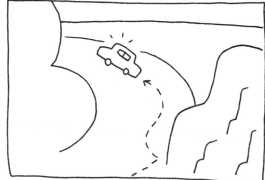

...BUT ANYONE WHO SAYS THEY
NEVER THINK ABOUT IT AGAIN IS LYING.

JENN

I still struggle with depression, but it's nothing like it was before.

I'm a happy person these days. My medication really helps.

 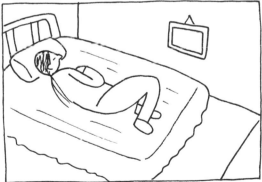

But if I feel I need to cancel my plans and stay
in bed all day, I will... and I apologize for that.

Tina

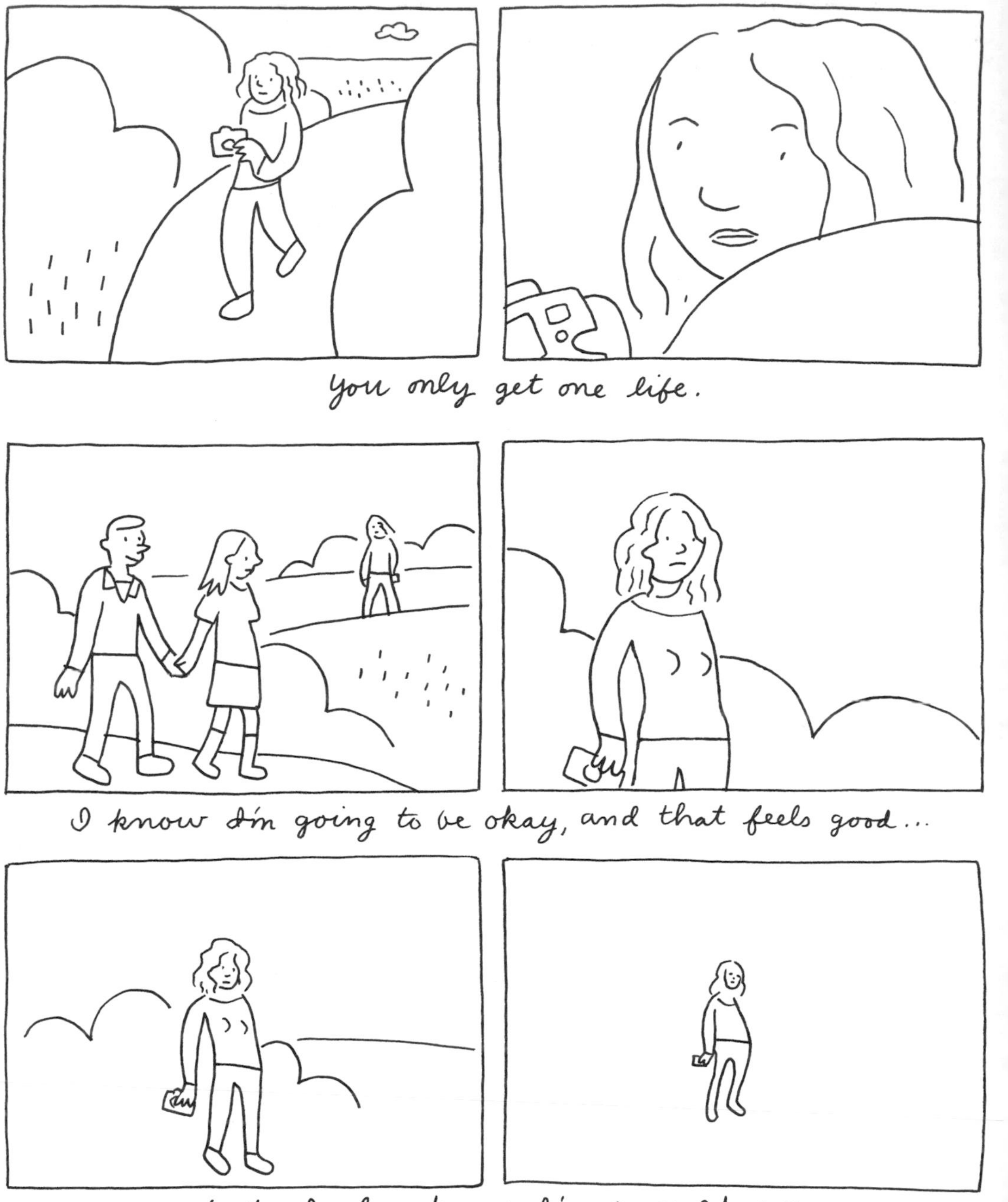
You only get one life.
I know I'm going to be okay, and that feels good...
...but I also know I'm screwed up,
and I may have to go back into the hospital again.
Chantel

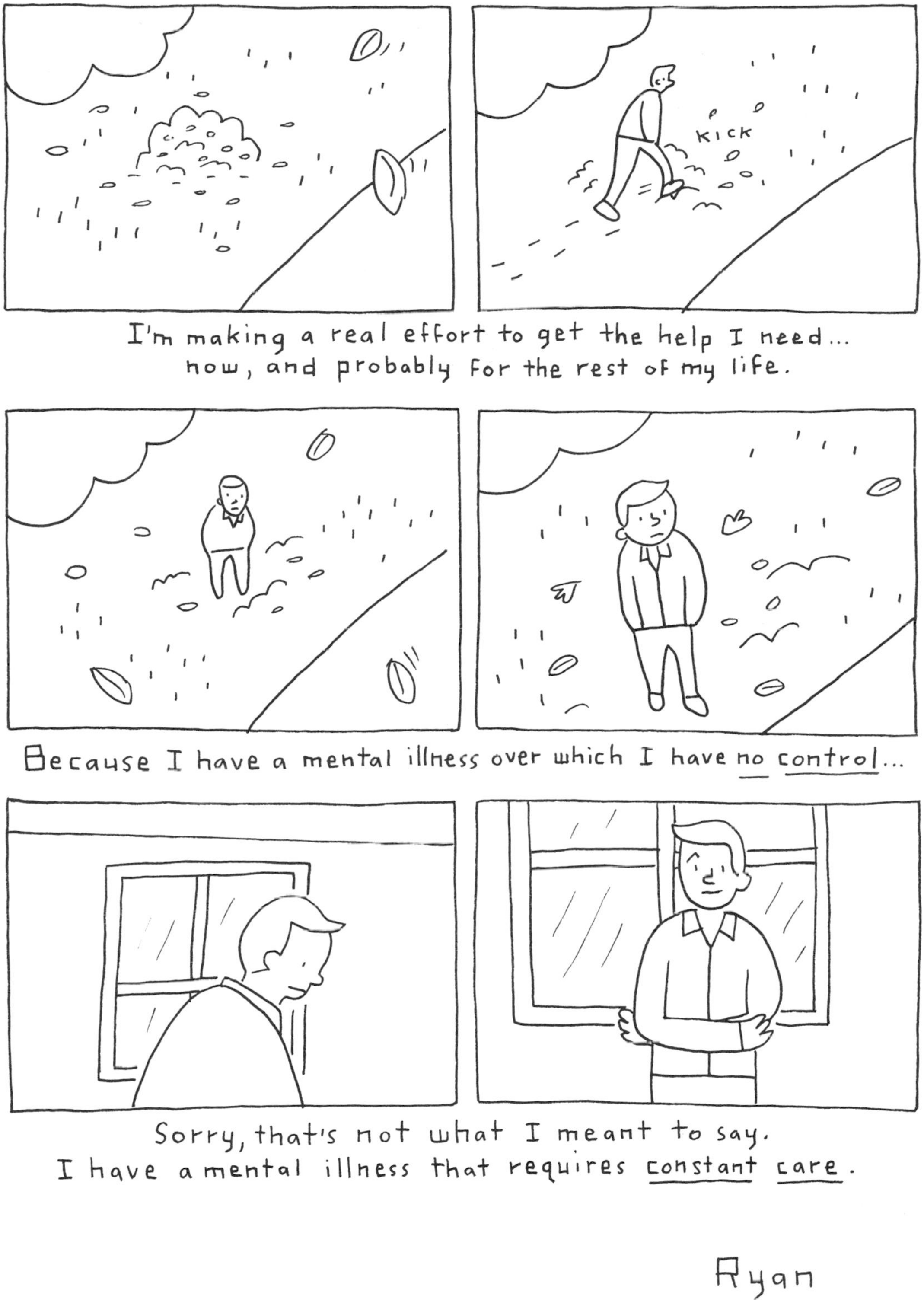
KICK
I'm making a real effort to get the help I need...
now, and probably for the rest of my life.
Because I have a mental illness over which I have no control...
Sorry, that's not what I meant to say.
I have a mental illness that requires constant care.
Ryan

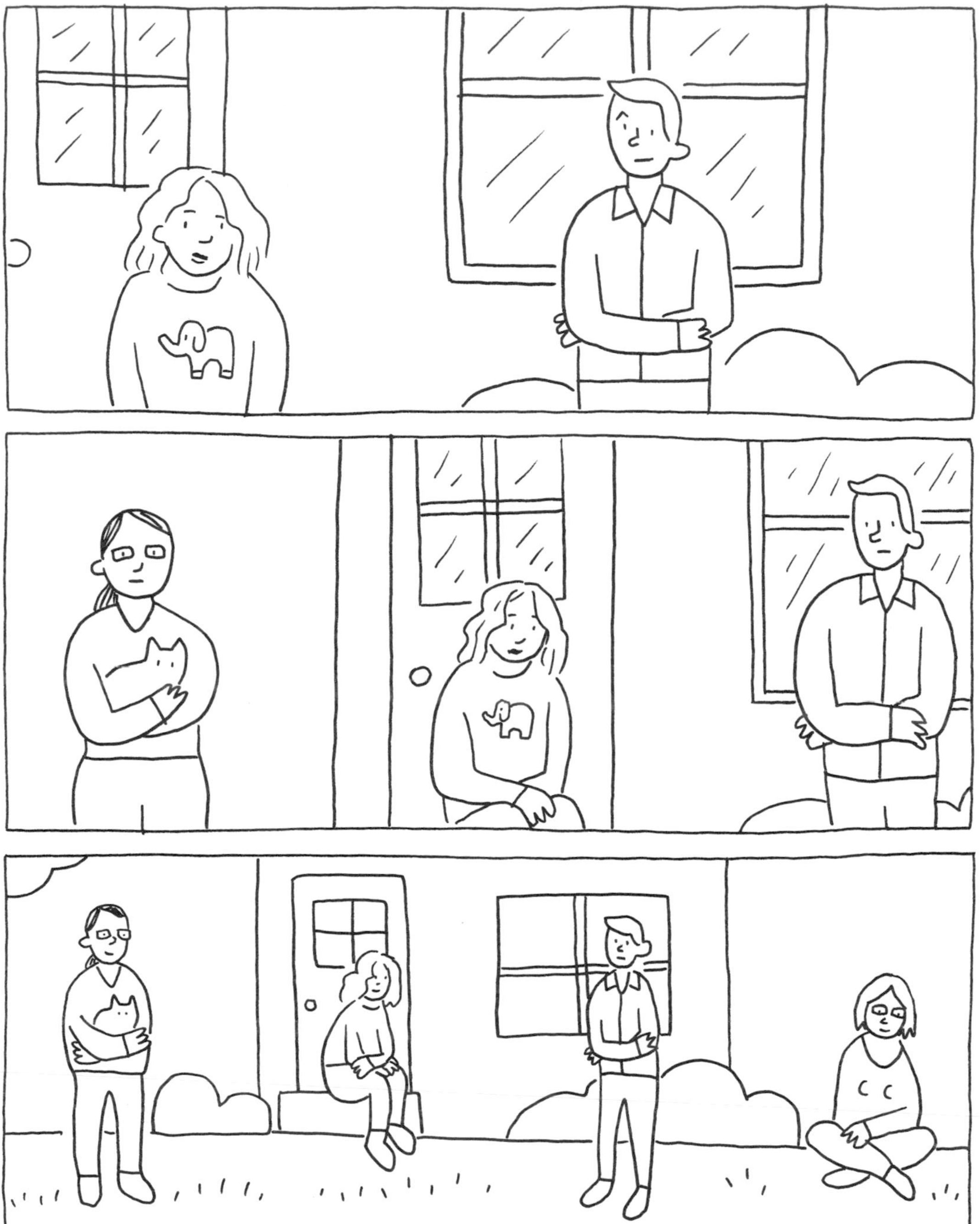

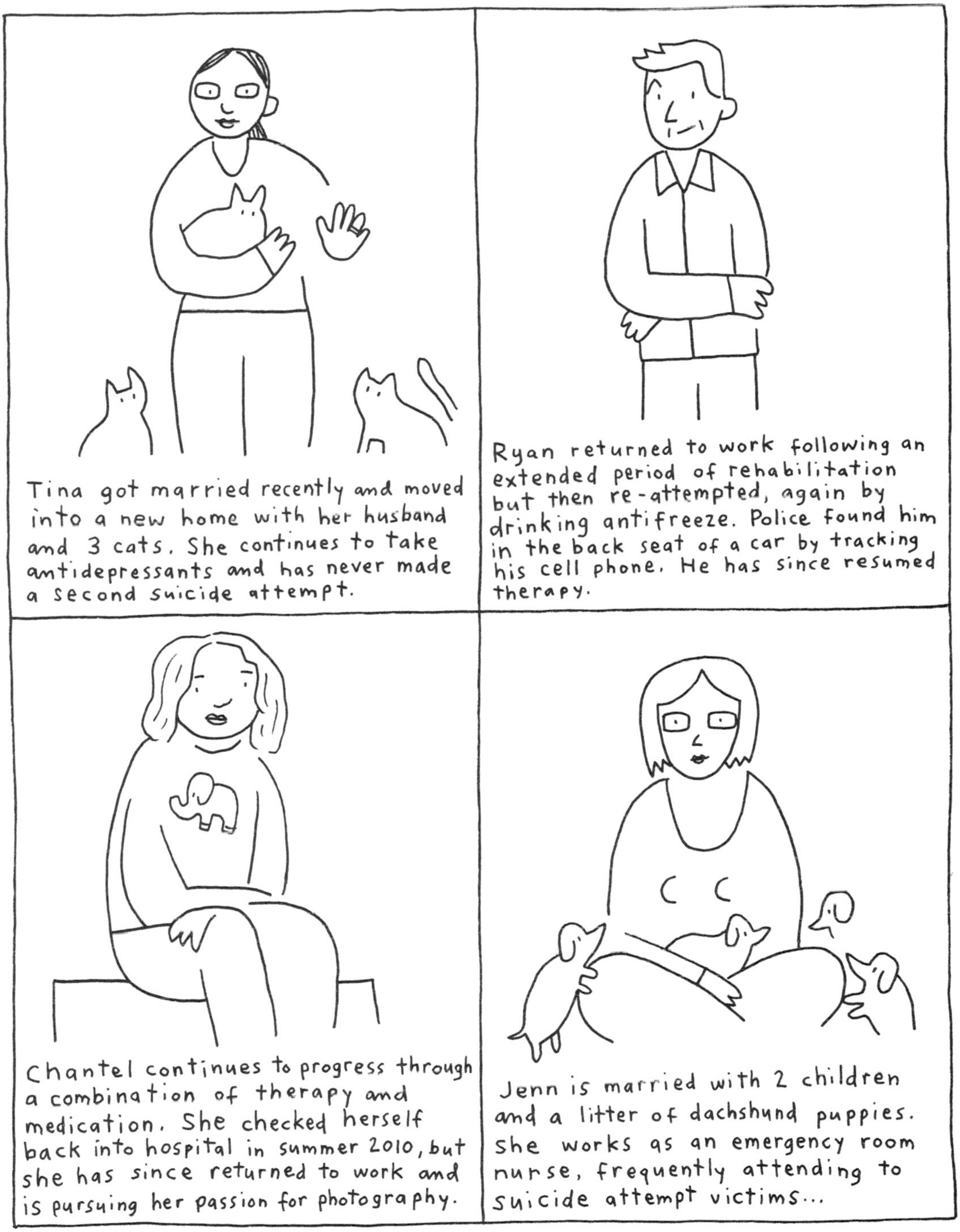
Tina got married recently and moved into a new home with her husband and 3 cats. She continues to take antidepressants and has never made a second suicide attempt.
Ryan returned to work following an extended period of rehabilitation but then re-attempted, again by drinking antifreeze. Police found him in the back seat of a car by tracking his cell phone. He has since resumed therapy.
Chantel continues to progress through a combination of therapy and medication. She checked herself back into hospital in summer 2010, but she has since returned to work and is pursuing her passion for photography.
Jenn is married with 2 children and a litter of dachshund puppies. She works as an emergency room nurse, frequently attending to suicide attempt victims...

SURVIVING A SUICIDE ATTEMPT HAS TO CHANGE YOU.

IT CHANGES EVERYTHING ABOUT YOU.

BECAUSE AT SOME POINT YOU HAVE TO COME TO
TERMS WITH A VERY SIMPLE FACT...

YOU ARE NOT MEANT TO BE DEAD.

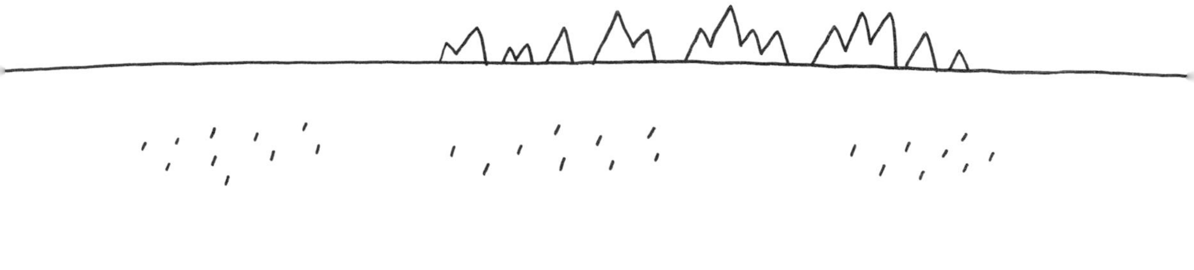

JENN

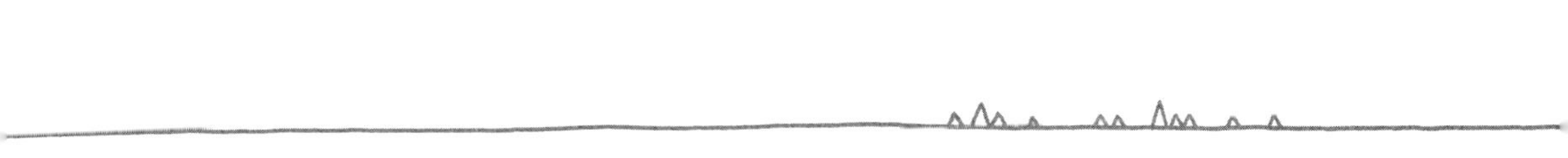

Alex Jansen   Jason Gilmore   Paul Peterson   John Porcellino

VERY SPECIAL THANKS

Chantel, Jenn, Ryan & Tina

The National Film Board of Canada

Written by
PAUL PETERSON &
JASON GILMORE

Illustrated by
JOHN PORCELLINO

Designed by
JASON GILMORE

Produced by
ALEX JANSEN, POP SANDBOX

Edited by
Richard Poplak & Alex Jansen

Copyediting and Proofreading by
Lorna Poplak

Developed from a traditional
documentary idea by
Paul Peterson

Original Documentary Interviews
written & Conducted by Paul Peterson
Shot & Directed by Jason Gilmore
Stills Photography by Sarah Cooper

Interactive Technical Lead
Brendan Hennessy

Mental Health Advisor
Michelle De Irish
(Research, Outreach & Consultation)

Marketing & Publicity
Alex Jansen
Ed Kanerva (Marketing Coordinator)
Dan Wagstaff (Raincoast Publicist)

Production Support
Alex MacGillivray
Audrey Quinn
Katie Parker
Lindsay Page
Michael Pontbriand
Sarah Joyce-Battersby
Sean Cartwright
Soo-Jin An

VISIT THE INTERACTIVE ONLINE EXPERIENCE
Co-produced by the National Film Board of Canada

nfb.ca/thenextday

THE NEXT DAY was simultaneously developed as an interactive online experience that allows viewers the opportunity to create their own path through the original audio interviews and features stunning animations based on the illustrations of John Porcellino.

The interactive experience is a co-production with the prestigious National Film Board of Canada (recipient of 70 Academy Award™ nominations) in association with TVO as part of the Calling Card Program.

Pop Sandbox is an award-winning multimedia production and publishing company with a focus on original projects rooted in graphic novel and film. It is a boutique operation centered on innovative and meaningful storytelling across platforms, from initial concept through production to eventual publication/distribution. Pop Sandbox aims to bring together artists from a variety of backgrounds and disciplines in a creative environment that fosters innovation in both content and form.

Pop Sandbox's inaugural release was KENK: A Graphic Portrait, the award-winning 300-page journalistic comic book surrounding "the world's most prolific bicycle thief" (The New York Times), which was recently named a Best Book of the Year by Quill & Quire (Canada's top literary magazine) and is being developed as a fully animated film.

SPECIAL THANKS & ACKNOWLEDGEMENTS

The CFC Media Lab
Chandra Halko
Christine McGlade & TVO
Craig Small
Jennifer Brasch &
The Reasons to Go On Living Project
Jenny Cooper
Julia Burns
Katie Parker
Lea Marin
Lisa Brown & Workman Arts
Paddy Laidley & Raincoast Books

Sarah Arruda
Scott Meyers & TVCOGECO Kingston
Shahid Quadri
Simone Rodrigue
Venicio Rebelo & Four Points
by Sheraton Kingston

Thank you to Nancy who has supported me through everything and my kids who always believed — Paul